Principles
in Practice

The Principles in Practice imprint offers teachers concrete illustrations of effective classroom practices based in NCTE research briefs and policy statements. Each book discusses the research on a specific topic, links the research to an NCTE brief or policy statement, and then demonstrates how those principles come alive in practice: by showcasing actual classroom practices that demonstrate the policies in action; by talking about research in practical, teacher-friendly language; and by offering teachers possibilities for rethinking their own practices in light of the ideas presented in the books. Books within the imprint are grouped in strands, each strand focused on a significant topic of interest.

Adolescent Literacy Strand

Adolescent Literacy at Risk? The Impact of Standards (2009) Rebecca Bowers Sipe

Adolescents and Digital Literacies: Learning Alongside Our Students (2010) Sara Kajder

Adolescent Literacy and the Teaching of Reading: Lessons for Teachers of Literature (2010) Deborah Appleman

Writing in Today's Classrooms Strand

Writing in the Dialogical Classroom: Students and Teachers Responding to the Texts of Their Lives (2011) Bob Fecho

Becoming Writers in the Elementary Classroom: Visions and Decisions (2011) Katie Van Sluys

Writing Instruction in the Culturally Relevant Classroom (2011) Maisha T. Winn and Latrise P. Johnson

Literacy Assessment Strand

Our Better Judgment: Teacher Leadership for Writing Assessment (2012) Chris W. Gallagher and Eric D. Turley

Beyond Standardized Truth: Improving Teaching and Learning through Inquiry-Based Reading Assessment (2012) Scott Filkins

Reading Assessment: Artful Teachers, Successful Students (2013) Diane Stephens, editor

Literacies of the Disciplines Strand

Entering the Conversations: Practicing Literacy in the Disciplines (2014) Patricia Lambert Stock, Trace Schillinger, and Andrew Stock

Real-World Literacies: Disciplinary Teaching in the High School Classroom (2014) Heather Lattimer

Doing and Making Authentic Literacies (2014) Linda Denstaedt, Laura Jane Roop, and Stephen Best

Reading in Today's Classrooms Strand

Connected Reading: Teaching Adolescent Readers in a Digital World (2015) Kristen Hawley Turner and Troy Hicks

Digital Reading: What's Essential in Grades 3–8 (2015) William L. Bass II and Franki Sibberson

Teaching Reading with YA Literature: Complex Texts, Complex Lives (2016) Jennifer Buehler

Teaching English Language Learners Strand

Beyond "Teaching to the Test": Rethinking Accountability and Assessment for English Language Learners (2017) Betsy Gilliland and Shannon Pella

Community Literacies en Confianza: *Learning from Bilingual After-School Programs* (2017) Steven Alvarez

Community Literacies *en Confianza*

Learning from Bilingual After-School Programs

Steven Alvarez
St. John's University

National Council of
Teachers of English

National Council of Teachers of English
1111 W. Kenyon Road, Urbana, Illinois 61801-1096

Staff Editor: Bonny Graham
Copy Editor: Susan Vargas-Sheltra
Series Editor: Cathy Fleischer
Interior Design: Victoria Pohlmann
Cover Design: Pat Mayer
Photos: cover, iStock/Feverpitched; p. 41, iStock/fstop123; p. 56, iStock/MarsBars; p. 83, iStock/dcdebs; all others by Steven Alvarez

NCTE Stock Number: 07867; eStock Number: 07874
ISBN 978-0-8141-0786-7; eISBN 978-0-8141-0787-4

Library of Congress Cataloging-in-Publication Data
Names: Alvarez, Steven, 1979- author.
Title: Community literacies en confianza : learning from bilingual after-school programs / Steven Alvarez.
Description: Urbana, IL : National Council of Teachers of English, 2017 | Includes bibliographical references and index.
Identifiers: LCCN 2017004533 (print) | LCCN 2017023826 (ebook) | ISBN 9780814107874 | ISBN 9780814107867 (pbk.)
Subjects: LCSH: Education, Bilingual—United States. | After-school programs—United States. | Culturally relevant pedagogy—United States. | Community and school—United States.
Classification: LCC LC3731 (ebook) | LCC LC3731 .A64 2047 (print) | DDC 370.117/50973—dc23
LC record available at https://lccn.loc.gov/2017004533

Contents

Acknowledgments

I first thank Valle del Bluegrass Library and the Kentucky United Latinos for allowing me to learn from you both. I've grown as a teacher because of you, and you have taught me how to appreciate my bilingual learning.

My colleagues from across the nation— Gustavo Arellano, Isabel Baca, Adam Banks, A. Suresh Canagarajah, Francisco Laguna Correa, John T. Edge, Nelson Flores, Laura Gonzales, Juan Guerra, David Kirkland, Rebecca Lorimer Leonard, Roxanne Mountford, Leigh Patel, R. Joseph Rodríguez, Mary P. Sheridan, and Kate Vieira—have offered friendship, wisdom, and advice for this work, and I thank you all. I also thank the Cultivating New Voices program of NCTE for instilling *confianza* among a committed group of scholars and friends. I send immense thanks to Cathy Fleischer for pushing me further with this work and my attention to prose.

I thank NCTE for publishing this book, and for including it in this series of fine books for teachers. Special thanks as well to the Woodrow Wilson National Fellowship Foundation's Career Enhancement Fellowship Program and the University of Kentucky for supporting the writing of this book.

In Chapter 7, I mention the mentors in my life: my first teachers, my parents, Mr. Robert and Mrs. Anna Alvarez of Safford, Arizona; and my schoolteachers, including Mrs. Smith at Dorothy Stinson Elementary School, Mr. MacDevitt at Lafe Nelson School, Mr. McKindles at Safford Middle School, Mrs. Lindsey at Safford High School, Dr. Hayot and Dr. Mountford at the University of Arizona, and Dr. Mlynarczyk and Dr. Shor at the Graduate Center of the City University of New York.

Finally, *gracias a mi* family for believing in me from the beginning. Thank you to *mis padres y mis hermanos* Tony, Fred, Debbie, and Nancy for reading with me early—in English and Spanish. I thank my partner, Sara Alvarez, for reading this work and for sharing many of these moments and a love for our communities.

NCTE Position Paper on the Role of English Teachers in Educating English Language Learners (ELLs)

Prepared by the NCTE ELL Task Force
Approved by the NCTE Executive Committee, April 2006

This position paper is designed to address the knowledge and skills mainstream teachers need to have in order to develop effective curricula that engage English language learners, develop their academic skills, and help them negotiate their identities as bilingual learners. More specifically, this paper addresses the language and literacy needs of these learners as they participate and learn in English-medium classes. NCTE has made clear bilingual students' right to maintain their native languages (see "On Affirming the CCCC 'Students' Right to Their Own Language'" 2003). Thus, this paper addresses ways teachers can help these students develop English as well as ways they can support their students' bilingualism. In the United States bilingual learners, more commonly referred to as English language learners, are defined as students who know a language other than English and are learning English. Students' abilities range from being non-English speakers to being fully proficient. The recommendations in this paper apply to all of them.

Context

The National Clearinghouse for English Language Acquisition (NCELA) reported that in 2003–04 there were over five million English language learners (ELLs) in schools in the United States (NCELA, 2004). In the last ten years the ELL population has grown 65%, and the diversity of those students continues to challenge teachers and schools. Although 82% of ELLs in the United States are native Spanish speakers, Hopstock and Stephenson (2003) found that school districts identified over 350 different first languages for their second language learners.

Federal, state, and local policies have addressed the education of bilingual learners by implementing different types of programs. Different models of bilingual education, English as a Second Language, English immersion, and integration into mainstream classes, sometimes referred to as submersion, are among the most common approaches. Preferences for the types of programs have changed over time, responding to demographic and political pressures. (For a historical and descriptive summary, see NCTE's "Position Statement on Issues in ESL and Bilingual Education"; Brisk, 2006; Crawford, 2004.)

The best way to educate bilingual learners has been at the center of much controversy. Research points to the advantage of quality bilingual programs (Greene, 1997; Ramirez, 1992; Rolstad, Mahoney, & Glass, 2005; Thomas & Collier, 2002; Willig, 1985) and the benefits of ESL instruction when language is taught through content (Freeman, Y. S., & Freeman, D. E., 1998; Marcia, 2000).

The Role of English Teachers in Educating ELLs

For a variety of reasons, however, the majority of ELLs find themselves in mainstream classrooms taught by teachers with little or no formal professional development in teaching such students (Barron & Menken, 2002; Kindler, 2002). Although improving the education of ELLs has been proposed as a pressing national educational priority (Waxman & Téllez, 2002), many teachers are not adequately prepared to work with a linguistically diverse student population (American Federation of Teachers, 2004; Fillmore & Snow, 2002; Gándara, Rumberger, Maxwell-Jolly, & Callahan, 2003; Menken & Antunez, 2001; Nieto, 2003).

Teachers working to better meet the needs of linguistically diverse students need support. NCTE encourages English teachers to collaborate and work closely with ESL and bilingual teaching professionals, who can offer classroom support, instructional advice, and general insights into second language acquisition. School administrators should support and encourage teachers to attend workshops and professional conferences that regularly offer sessions on bilingual learners, particularly in the areas of reading and writing. Schools should also consider seeking professional development for their teachers from neighboring colleges.

In turn, colleges and universities providing teacher education should offer all preservice teachers, as well as teachers pursuing advanced degree work, preparation in teaching linguistically diverse learners in their future classrooms. Coursework should be offered on second language writing and reading, and on second language acquisition, as well as on culture, and should be encouraged for all teachers.

Who Are the Students?

Bilingual students differ in various ways, including level of oral English proficiency, literacy ability in both the heritage language and English, and cultural backgrounds. English language learners born in the United States often develop conversational language abilities in English but lack academic language proficiency. Newcomers, on the other hand, need to develop both conversational and academic English. Education previous to entering U.S. schools helps determine students' literacy levels in their native language. Some learners may have age-/grade-level skills, while others have limited or no literacy because of the quality of previous schooling, interrupted schooling due to wars or migration, and other circumstances (Suárez-Orozco & Suárez-Orozco, 2001). Given the wide range of English language learners and their backgrounds, it is important that all teachers take the time to learn about their students, particularly in terms of their literacy histories.

Immigrant students and the children of immigrants in the United States come from many cultural backgrounds. The background knowledge English learners bring to school greatly affects their performance. For this reason, teachers of English language learners should be sure to build background for content lessons rather than assuming that bilingual students come with the same background knowledge as mainstream students.

Teaching Bilingual Learners in Mainstream Classrooms

This section specifically addresses teaching language, reading, and writing, as well as the specific kinds of academic literacy that are often a part of most English and language arts curricula. Although English language arts teachers have literacy as the focus of their teaching, many of these suggestions are useful for teachers working in the content areas as well. To acquire academic content through English, English language learners need to learn English. The academic language that students need in the different content areas differs, and students need scaffolding to help them to learn both the English language and the necessary content. For English language learners, teachers need to consider content objectives as well as English language development objectives.

Bilinguals need three types of knowledge to become literate in a second language. They need to know the second language; they need to know literacy; and they need world knowledge (Bernhardt, 1991). The sections below list key ideas for helping English language learners develop academic English proficiency. More detailed information on the topics covered in this section can be obtained from the topical bibliography compiled as part of this project.

To teach bilingual learners, teachers must get to know their learners.

Knowledge of the Students

Knowledge of the students is key to good teaching. Because teachers relate to students both as learners and as children or adolescents, teachers must establish how they will address these two types of relationships, what they need to know about their students, and how they will acquire this knowledge. The teacher-learner relationship implies involvement between teachers and students around subject matter and language and literacy proficiency in both languages. Adult-child relationships are more personal and should include the family. Focusing on both types of relationships bridges the gap between school and the world outside it, a gap that is especially important for many bilingual students whose world differs greatly from school.

Teaching Language

Second language learners need to develop academic proficiency in English to master content-area subjects. Teachers can provide effective instruction for these students by:

- Recognizing that second language acquisition is a gradual developmental process and is built on students' knowledge and skill in their native language;
- Providing authentic opportunities to use language in a nonthreatening environment;
- Teaching key vocabulary connected with the topic of the lesson;
- Teaching academic oral language in the context of various content areas;
- Teaching text- and sentence-level grammar in context to help students understand the structure and style of the English language;
- Teaching the specific features of language students need to communicate in social as well as academic contexts.

The Role of English Teachers in Educating ELLs

Teaching Literacy: Reading

Bilingual students also need to learn to read and write effectively in order to succeed in school.

Teachers can support English language learners' literacy development by:

- Introducing classroom reading materials that are culturally relevant;
- Connecting the readings with the students' background knowledge and experiences;
- Encouraging students to discuss the readings, including the cultural dimensions of the text;
- Having students read a more accessible text on the topic before reading the assigned text;
- Asking families to read with students a version in the heritage language;
- Replacing discrete skill exercises and drills with many opportunities to read;
- Providing opportunities for silent reading in either the students' first language or in English;
- Reading aloud frequently to allow students to become familiar with and appreciate the sounds and structures of written language;
- Reading aloud while students have access to the text to facilitate connecting oral and written modalities;
- Stimulating students' content knowledge of the text before introducing the text;
- Teaching language features, such as text structure, vocabulary, and text- and sentence-level grammar to facilitate comprehension of the text;
- Recognizing that first and second language growth increases with abundant reading and writing.

Support reading comprehension by:

- Relating the topic to the cultural experiences of the students;
- "Front loading" comprehension via a walk through the text or a preview of the main ideas, and other strategies that prepare students for the topic of the text;
- Having students read a more accessible text on the topic before reading the assigned text;
- Asking families to read with students a version in the heritage language;
- Doing pre-reading activities that elicit discussion of the topic;
- Teaching key vocabulary essential for the topic;
- Recognizing that experiences in writing can be used to clarify understanding of reading.

Teaching Literacy: Writing

Writing well in English is often the most difficult skill for English language learners to master. Many English language learners are still acquiring vocabulary and syntactic competence in their writing. Students may show varying degrees of acquisition, and not all second language writers will have the same difficulties or challenges. Teachers should be aware that English language learners may not be familiar with terminology and routines often associated with writing instruction in the United States, including writing process, drafting, revision, editing, workshop, conference, audience, purpose, or genre. Furthermore, certain elements of discourse, particularly in terms of audience and persuasion, may differ across cultural contexts. The same is true for textual borrowing and plagiarism. The CCCC Statement on Second Language Writing and Writers is a useful resource for all teachers of writing to examine.

Teachers can provide instructional support for English language learners in their writing by:

- Providing a nurturing environment for writing;
- Introducing cooperative, collaborative writing activities which promote discussion;
- Encouraging contributions from all students, and promoting peer interaction to support learning;
- Replacing drills and single-response exercises with time for writing practice;
- Providing frequent meaningful opportunities for students to generate their own texts;
- Designing writing assignments for a variety of audiences, purposes, and genres, and scaffolding the writing instruction;
- Providing models of well-organized papers for the class. Teachers should consider glossing sample papers with comments that point to the specific aspects of the paper that make it well written;
- Offering comments on the strength of the paper, in order to indicate areas where the student is meeting expectations;
- Making comments explicit and clear (both in written response and in oral responses). Teachers should consider beginning feedback with global comments (content and ideas, organization, thesis) and then move on to more local concerns (or mechanical errors) when student writers are more confident with the content of their draft;
- Giving more than one suggestion for change—so that students still maintain control of their writing;
- Not assuming that every learner understands how to cite sources or what plagiarism is. Teachers should consider talking openly about citation and plagiarism in class, exploring the cultural values that are implicit in the rules of plagiarism and textual borrowing, and noting that not all cultures ascribe to the same rules and guidelines. Students should be provided with strategies for avoiding plagiarism.

Teaching Language and Content

The best way to help students learn both English and the knowledge of school subjects is to teach language through content. This should not replace reading and writing instruction in English, nor study of literature and grammar. There are three key reasons to do this:

1. **Students get both language and content.**
   Research has shown that students can learn English and subject matter content material

at the same time. Students don't need to delay the study of science or literature until they reach high levels of English. Instead, they can learn both simultaneously. Given the time limitations older students face, it is crucial that classes provide them with both academic content-area knowledge and academic English.

2. **Language is kept in its natural context.**
   When teachers teach science in English, students learn science terms as they study biology or chemistry. The vocabulary occurs naturally as students read and discuss science texts.

3. **Students have reasons to use language for real purposes.**
   The primary purpose of school is to help students develop the knowledge of different academic disciplines. When academic content is presented in English, students focus on the main purpose of schooling: learning science, math, social studies, or literature. In the process, they also learn English.

Selecting Materials

- Choose a variety of texts around a theme.
- Choose texts at different levels of difficulty.
- Choose reading and writing materials that represent the cultures of the students in the class.
- When possible, include texts in the native languages of the ELLs in the class. The following considerations should be used as a guide for choosing texts that support bilingual learners:
  - Materials should include both literature and informational texts.
  - Materials should include culturally relevant texts.
  - Authentic materials should be written to inform or entertain, not to teach a grammar point or a letter-sound correspondence.
  - The language of the text should be natural.
  - If translated, the translation should be good language.
  - Materials should include predictable text for emergent readers.
  - Materials should include texts with nonlinguistic cues that support comprehension (For a more comprehensive checklist, see Freeman, Y. S., & Freeman, D. E., 2002; Freeman, D. E., & Freeman, Y. S., 2004).

Low-Level Literacy Immigrant Students

Late-arrival immigrant and refugee students with low literacy skills have been found to benefit from Newcomer programs or Welcome Centers designed for 1–3 semesters of high school (Boyson & Short, 2003; Schnur, 1999; Short, 2002). The focus is to help students acquire beginning English skills and guide students' acculturation to the U.S. school system before enrollment in regular ESL language support programs or content-area classrooms. The integration of such programs in high school English departments should be encouraged.

Conclusion

As the number of bilingual learners in mainstream classes increases, it becomes even more important for mainstream teachers to use effective practices to engage these students so that they can acquire the academic English and the content-area knowledge they need for school success. The guidelines offered here are designed as initial suggestions for teachers to follow. However, we recognize that all teachers need much more. Teachers need continued support and professional development to enable all their students, including their bilingual students, to succeed.

References

American Federation of Teachers. (March, 2004). *Closing the achievement gap: Focus on Latino students* (Policy Brief 17). Retrieved March 28, 2006, from http://www.aft.org/teachers/pusbs-reports/index.htm#english.

Barron, V., & Menken, K. (2002). *What are the characteristics of the bilingual education and ESL teacher shortage?* Washington, D.C.: National Clearinghouse for English Language Acquisition and Language Instruction Educational Programs.

Bernhardt, E. B. (1991). A psycholinguistic perspective on second language literacy. Reading in Two Languages. *AILA Review, 8*, 31–44.

Boyson, B. A., & Short, D. J. (2003). *Secondary school newcomer programs in the United States* (Research Report 12). Santa Cruz, CA, and Washington, DC: Center for Research on Education Diversity & Excellence.

Brisk, M. E. (2006). *Bilingual education: From compensatory to quality schooling.* (2nd ed.) Mahwah, NJ: Erlbaum.

Crawford, J. (2004). *Educating English learners.* Los Angeles: Bilingual Education Services.

De Jong, E. J. (2002). Effective bilingual education: From theory to academic achievement in a two-way bilingual program. *Bilingual Research Journal, 26*(1), 1–15.

Fillmore, L. W., & Snow, C. (2002). What teachers need to know about language. In C. T. Adger, C. Snow, & D. Christian (Eds.), *What teachers need to know about language* (pp. 7–53). Washington, DC: Center for Applied Linguistics.

Freeman, D. E., and Freeman, Y. S. (2004). *Essential linguistics: What you need to know to teach reading, ESL, spelling, phonics, and grammar.* Portsmouth, NH: Heinemann.

Freeman, Y. S., & Freeman, D. E. (1998). *ESL/EFL teaching: Principles for success.* Portsmouth, NH: Heinemann.

Freeman, Y. S., and Freeman, D. E. (2002). *Closing the achievement gap.* Portsmouth, NH: Heinemann.

Gándara, P., Rumberger, R., Maxwell-Jolly, J., & Callahan, R. (2003). English learners in California schools: Unequal resources, unequal outcomes. *Education Policy Analysis Archives, 11*(36). Retrieved March 28, 2006, from http://epaa.asu.edu/.

Gibbons, P. (2002). *Scaffolding language, scaffolding learning: Teaching second language learners in the mainstream classroom.* Portsmouth, NH: Heinemann.

Greene, J. P. (1997). A meta-analysis of the Rossell and Baker review of bilingual education research. *Bilingual Research Journal, 21.*

The Role of English Teachers in Educating ELLs

Hopstock, P. & Stephenson, T. (2003). *Native languages of limited English proficient students*. U.S. Department of Education. Retrieved March 5, 2006.

Kindler, A. L. (2002). *Survey of the states' limited English proficient students and available educational programs and services 1999–2000 summary report*. Washington, DC: National Clearinghouse for English Language Acquisition and Language Instruction Education Programs (NCELA). Retrieved Dec. 26, 2003, from http://www.ncela.gwu.edu.

Krashen, S. (1996). *Under attack: The case against bilingual education*. Culver City, CA: Language Education Associates.

McQuillan, J., & Tse, L. (1997). Does research matter? An analysis of media opinion of bilingual education, 1984–1994. *Bilingual Research Journal, 20*(1), 1–27.

Menken, K., & Antunez, B. (2001). *An overview of the preparation and certification of teachers working with limited English proficient students*. Washington, DC: National Clearinghouse of Bilingual Education. Retrieved July 28, 2003, from http://www.ericsp.org/pages/digests/ncbe.pdf.

NCELA. (2006). *The growing number of limited English proficient students 1991–2002*. Washington, DC: U.S. Department of Education.

Nieto, S. M. (2003). *What keeps teachers going?* New York: Teachers College.

Pally, M. (Ed.) (2000). *Sustained content teaching in academic ESL/EFL: A practical approach*. Boston: Houghton Mifflin.

Ramirez, J. D. (1992). Executive summary. *Bilingual Research Journal, 16*, 1–62.

Rolstad, K., Mahoney, K., & Glass, G. V. (2005) The big picture: A meta-analysis of program effectiveness research on English language learners. *Educational Policy, 19*, 572–594.

Schnur, B. (1999). A newcomer's high school. *Educational Leadership, 56*(7), 50–52.

Short, D. J. (2002). Newcomer programs: An educational alternative for secondary immigrant students. *Education and Urban Society 34*(2), 173–198.

Solomon, J., & Rhodes, N. (1995). *Conceptualizing academic language*. Washington, DC: The National Center for Research on Cultural Diversity and Second Language Learning.

Suárez-Orozco, C., & Suárez-Orozco, M. M. (2001). *Children of immigration*. Cambridge, MA: Harvard University.

Thomas, W. P., & Collier, V. P. (2002). *A national study of school effectiveness for language minority students' long-term academic achievement*. Santa Cruz, CA: Center for Research on Education, Diversity & Excellence, University of California, Santa Cruz.

Waxman, H. C., & Téllez, K. (2002). *Research synthesis on effective teaching practices for English language learners* (Publication Series No. 3). Philadelphia: Mid-Atlantic Regional Educational Laboratory.

Willig, A. C. (1985). A meta-analysis of selected studies on the effectiveness of bilingual education. *Review of Educational Research, 55*(3), 269–317.

For more resources to support English language learners, see http://www.ncte.org/positions/statements/teacherseducatingell.

Statement of Terminology and Glossary

Steven Alvarez, St. John's University

Betsy Gilliland, University of Hawai`i Mānoa

Christina Ortmeier-Hooper, University of New Hampshire

Melinda J. McBee Orzulak, Bradley University

Shannon Pella, California State University, Sacramento

As authors of the various books in the Teaching English Language Learners strand of the NCTE Principles in Practice (PIP) imprint, we have made a concerted effort to use consistent terminology in these volumes. All of us have thought long and hard about the ways in which we label and describe bilingual and ELL students and the programs that often provide these students with additional support. Even so, readers will notice some variation in terms used to describe students, classrooms, and teaching practices. The concern over terminology is part of a long-standing discussion and trends in the labeling of these students, as well as of the fields that conduct research on teachers and students working across languages to teach and learn English. Often the shifting among terms leads to confusion and contention for teachers, administrators, teacher educators, and policymakers.

To address this confusion and tension, we begin each book in this strand with a glossary of common terms and acronyms that are part of current discussions about meeting the needs of these students in English language arts classrooms and beyond. For many readers, the terms themselves and the ongoing shift to new terms can be alienating, the jargon dividing readers into insiders and outsiders. But often the shift in terms has a great deal to do with both policy and issues of identity for students. For example, up until the No Child Left Behind (NCLB) Act of 2001, most educational documents referred to these students as *bilingual* or *ESL*, both of which acknowledge that English is a second language and that a student has a first language as well.

The term *English language learner* was adopted with NCLB and brought into our schools and the larger public discourse. In fact, in 2002 the US Department of Education renamed the Office of Bilingual Education and Minority Languages Affairs. It became the Office of English Language Acquisition, Language Enhancement and Academic Achievement for Limited English Proficient Students, now identified simply as the Office of English Language Acquisition (OELA). The change indicated a shift away from acknowledging students' home languages or bilingual abilities. Close to two decades later, the term *English language learner* remains prominent in educational policy and in many textbooks geared toward teachers and teacher educators. Its prominence and familiarity in the literature makes it an accessible way to talk about these students. Yet, as we have heard from many students through the years, the term *English language learner* can also be limiting. As one student asked, "When do I stop being an English language learner and get to just be an English language user?" The term also works against efforts to acknowledge the competencies and linguistically sophisticated talents these students have as translators, bilingual speakers, and cross-cultural negotiators.

Statement of Terminology and Glossary

In these PIP volumes, we use the term *English language learner* as a way to reach out to readers who see and hear this term regularly used in their schools, in their hallways, and in other helpful books in the field. However, some of us also use the terms *multilingual* or *bilingual* in order to encourage a discussion of these young people not simply as novice English learners but as individuals with linguistic and academic competencies they have gained from bilingual/multilingual experiences and literacies.

Glossary

Bilingual, multilingual, or plurilingual: These terms refer to the ability to use (i.e., speak, write, and/or read) multiple languages. For many ELL-designated students in US schools, English is actually the third or fourth language they have learned, making *bilingual* not necessarily an accurate term.

Emergent bilingual: This term has been proposed as a more appropriate term than *LEP* or *ELL*, because it points to possibilities of developing bilingualism rather than focusing on language limits or deficiencies (García, 2009).

English as a foreign language (EFL): Refers to non-native English-speaking students who are learning English in a country where English is not the primary language.

English as an international language (EIL) or English as a lingua franca (ELF): These are terms used to refer to global conceptions of English, or English used for communication between members of various nations.

English as a second language (ESL): Readers may be most familiar with this term because it has been used as an overarching term for students, programs, and/or a field of study. Currently the term usually refers to programs of instruction (i.e., study of English in an English-speaking country); however, *ESL* was used in the past to refer to English language learning students.

English language learner (ELL): In keeping with the terminology used in the *NCTE Position Paper on the Role of English Teachers in Educating English Language Learners (ELLs)*, this PIP strand employs the term *ELL*, which is commonly used in secondary schools as the short form of *English language learner*. The term refers to a complex, heterogeneous range of students who are in the process of learning English.

English learner (EL): This is the preferred term of the California Department of Education (and, increasingly, other states). California is the state with the largest number and percentage of emergent bilingual students enrolled in public schools. Over the past twenty years, California has moved from *LEP* to *ELL* and, most recently, from *ELL* to *EL*.

First language (L1) and second language (L2): *L1* has been used to refer to students' "mother tongue" or "home language" as they learn additional languages (referred to as *L2*).

Generation 1.5: This term, originally used in higher education, often refers to students who have been long-term residents in the United States but who were born abroad (al-

Statement of Terminology and Glossary

though the term is sometimes also used to refer to US-born children of recent immigrants). The designation of 1.5 describes their feelings of being culturally between first- and second-generation immigrants; they are often fluent in spoken English but may still be working to command aspects of written English, especially academic writing. As long-term residents, these students may reject *ESL* as a term that has been used to refer to recent immigrants to the United States.

Limited English proficiency (LEP): This abbreviation may be used in some educational contexts to refer to a designation used by the US Department of Education. Many scholars see this as a deficit term because of its focus on subtractive language (language that implies a deficiency) under a monolingual assumption of proficiency.

Long-term English language learner (LTELL): Currently in use in some states, this term refers to K–12 students who have been enrolled in US schools for many years and continue to be stuck with the ELL designation long past the time it should take for redesignation. Like Generation 1.5 students, LTELLs may have spent most if not all of their education in US schools. For a variety of reasons, including family mobility, inconsistent educational programs, and personal reasons, they have not had opportunities to learn academic language sufficiently to pass English language proficiency tests and other measures of proficiency for redesignation (Olsen, 2010).

Mainstream: This term is increasingly antiquated due to shifting demographics in the United States. In practice, it often refers to nonremedial, nonhonors, nonsheltered classes and programs. Sometimes it is used to refer to native or monolingual English speakers as a norm; changing demographics, however, mean that schools increasingly have a majority of culturally and linguistically diverse students, so it's been argued that a linguistically diverse classroom is the "New Mainstream" (Enright, 2011).

Monolingual: This term is used to refer to people who speak only one language, although often this label masks speakers' fluent use of multiple dialects, or variations, of English—an issue of particular concern when working with culturally diverse students who use other varieties of English (such as Hawai'i Pidgin or African American Vernacular) in their lives outside of school. The monolingual English label can mask these diverse students' need to learn academic English just as much as their immigrant classmates do. Much of what this PIP strand discusses is relevant to students who utilize multiple varieties of English; teachers can support these students by acknowledging their multilingualism and helping them learn to use English for academic and other purposes.

Native or non-native English speakers (NES, NNES): Some materials contrast native English speakers (NES) with non-native English speakers (NNES). As with *monolingual*, the term *native speaker* is increasingly unclear, given how many long-term ELLs speak English fluently without a "foreign" accent and yet technically have another world language as their home or first language.

Newcomer: Some school districts have separate one-year programs for "newcomers," or students who are newly arrived in the United States, in which students learn not just "surviv-

Statement of Terminology and Glossary

al" English, but also how school works in the United States. As the position statement discusses, it's sometimes argued that newcomer programs benefit "low-level literacy immigrant students" and/or students with interrupted formal education who may have limited literacy in their first language (L1). Other newcomers may be fully literate in L1, especially by high school, and may or may not benefit from being isolated from the mainstream curriculum. For older students, the challenge is to move away from "low-level" ideas of literacy assessment that may discount the literacies of these students.

Resident or local bilingual, multilingual, or plurilingual: These terms are sometimes used to refer to students who reside in the United States (in contrast to those who are on student visas). Resident students may or may not be US citizens, others may not have permanent resident status, while still others may not have immigration documentation at all.

References

Enright, K. A. (2011). Language and literacy for a new mainstream. *American Educational Research Journal, 48*(1), 80–118. doi: 10.3102/0002831210368989

García, O. (2009). Emergent bilinguals and TESOL: What's in a name? *TESOL Quarterly, 43*(2), 322–26. doi:10.1002/j.1545-7249.2009.tb00172.x

Olsen, L. (2010). *Reparable harm: Fulfilling the unkept promise of educational opportunity for California's long term English learners*. Long Beach, CA: Californians Together.

Chapter One

Community Literacy Pedagogies: From a Translingual View

Sixteen-year-old Kevin,[1] who was originally born in Mexico but had lived in Kentucky for most of his life, remembered learning English with the Kentucky United Latinos (KUL, pronounced "cool") bilingual after-school group when he was younger. In an autobiographical piece of writing he read during a KUL meeting, Kevin described his early literacy struggles in elementary school and how he had overcome them to thrive as a bilingual student:

> I remember when I started school in the US and had to read English in front of the class, *y no hablaba inglés* [and I did not speak English]. My heart dropped because I just started school four months previously, so I still only knew a few words. The teacher didn't know I didn't know how to speak English. Everybody started laughing. *No le entendí* [I did not understand her]. Yeah, *eso me hizo enojado* [that made me upset] so that I started to read out loud and slightly right. *Estaba practicando y practicando.* [I was practicing and practicing.] From that day on, I said to myself that I was not that bad, so I started to try my hardest to learn English and do my best in every class. Now look at me in high school and reading like never before.

Kevin's traumatic memory of this "round-robin"-style class read-aloud as he was just learning English represented a common experience among bilingual students in the KUL after-school group. Indeed, researchers point out that such teaching practices too often shame and alienate students learning English (Opitz and Guccione). The memory of class "read-arounds" left several other KUL members feeling humiliated in front of classmates, but many, like Kevin, used the event as inspiration to work harder, to practice, as they learned English.

Kevin was representative of many of the after-school students as he occupied a space between English and Spanish. Kevin admitted that he now reads and writes better in English and uses Spanish "when I'm talking to my mom or family, but hardly at all to write." Kevin, like other KUL students, also admitted that sometimes older members of his family and community said he would lose his Mexican identity if he did not use Spanish more.

Such ethnic identity questions can cause stress, and stress caused by language differences can indeed affect relationships between not only family members but communities, as well. For emergent bilingual youth, perceptions of negative status attached to their home languages can push them to disidentify from their bilingualism with peers and in school in favor of speaking like a monolingual so-called "native." And yet, because of their backgrounds, this push can be problematic. Fourteen-year-old KUL member Ana wrote about her disappointment in not feeling "authentic" like a monolingual Mexican Spanish or American English speaker:

> When I began school and interacted with English speakers, they would assume I spoke only Spanish. I never felt bad about that, and it would actually make me feel happy, like I was more Mexican even though my Spanish wasn't that great. *Tengo pena* [I am ashamed] because of my so-so Spanish. All my family speaks it, but I can't spell correctly in Spanish, and when I try to speak it, I tend to add English words. I mix them a lot too. I struggle to express myself correctly due to not being able to find the right words. I don't have this problem as much in English, though.

It was clear to Ana that because of her appearance, people assumed she could not speak English, at least not like a monolingual English speaker. But she also felt judged because of her lack of fluency in Spanish, particularly when it came to orthography and spelling. Like Kevin, Ana attached language to identity and used different languages, depending on the context and audience.

Even if she mostly expressed herself in English, Ana noted that she thought bilingually: "I mix them a lot too." Her movement across languages was influenced by considerations of audience, vocabulary, definitions, synonyms, and word choices; yet, like many creative and intelligent students, she would not give herself credit for her ability to use two languages. Instead, she compared herself with her monolingual classmates, despite the fact that she was not a monolingual student.

These insights from Kevin and Ana are important, not only because they demonstrate how emergent bilingual students transition to writing exclusively in English, but also because they illustrate the ways in which students strive to learn English, even at the expense of the gifts of their home languages. No doubt, this pursuit of monolingual-level proficiency in English literacy overshadowed their bilingual gifts.

Both students were able to share their experiences with the KUL after-school group, and thus to find a community of students and teachers who cared. Kevin and Ana used Spanish openly with KUL members and did not feel alienated because of their bilingual tendencies. In interviews, they described their growing confidence with English and how their language struggles marked them as different when they were confronted with monolingual audiences, whether Spanish- or English-speaking. Their stories remind teachers why it is important to listen to students, and to empower them by providing opportunities to share stories in communities of trust. Eliciting these stories is one of the most powerful aims of a literacy pedagogy that demonstrates care for students and honors the voices and lived experiences of individuals and communities in all languages. Cultivating a caring atmosphere in multiple languages, however, requires additional effort, guidance, and trust-building between teachers and communities.

It takes a community to raise a bilingual child. This assertion does not overstate the collective project of nurturing bilingualism: the *NCTE Position Paper on the Role of English Teachers in Educating English Language Learners* (reprinted at the front of this book) emphasizes that to be sensitive to the language and literacy needs of their emergent bilingual students, K–12 teachers must learn about students' families and communities while establishing connections of trust. This brief challenges K–12 language arts teachers to discover an orientation to literacy that removes barriers between languages, an orientation that recognizes the gifts of emergent bilingual students with assignments that engage their bilingual abilities. Such engaging assignments advance critical academic skills and support students' bilingual practices with sensitivity to their identities and communities. Our literacy pedagogies, therefore, must include openness to learning from students' communities—that is, "to teach bilingual learners, teachers must get to know their learners" (*English Language Learners* 4). Students come to the classroom with abilities to use all their languages in creative and important ways. How teachers approach these abilities depends on their research and use of "culturally relevant materials to build on students' linguistic and cultural resources, while teaching language through content and themes" (*English Language Learners* 4). I agree completely with the brief, but I challenge educators—including myself—to extend these ideas even further to develop a pedagogy that affirms emergent bilingual students' lived experiences. Learning about students' communities means investigating where and how communities make spaces for themselves and for their voices to be heard. Indeed, the communities of our students are speaking, and we, as teachers, must always listen—even if the home languages they speak are not our own.

Before I move too much further, I have to offer a definition of what I mean by *community*. I define community as social inclusion based on interaction with other people, and a sense of social belonging through meaningful modes of involvement. Community involves both social and subjective feelings, and belonging can mean different things for different members. Community members can be motivated by any number of commonalities to align, organize spaces, and share interests. Schools are important community spaces, vital both for language learning and for raising community awareness of the power of literacy and social involvement.

I focus in this book on ethnographic case studies of two communities of students and families, KUL and Valle del Bluegrass Library (VBL). The communities are composed of emergent bilingual students and parents learning about schools as they learn English—in the case of VBL, students from preK to middle school, and in the case of KUL, high school students. The two communities illustrate how parents, teachers, and local volunteers in two different contexts organize around meeting schoolwork needs. In KUL and VBL, emergent bilingual students and their families collectively navigate school systems and the English language with the help of after-school programs and their networks of members, teachers, and volunteers. I draw upon my experiences with KUL and VBL to create portraits of bilingual after-school communities that offer relatable examples of how schools and teachers can partner and draw from community learning. I also explore what lessons we can draw from these portraits that could influence how we teach writing in school. This central focus on community, highlighted in NCTE's *The Role of English Teachers in Educating English Language Learners*, puts the local knowledge and experiences of students and families in the forefront, and offers insight and hope for the future of such collaborations.

In this book, I argue that K–12 English language arts teachers must expand their knowledge of the literacy practices of English language learners by engaging with their students' communities, learning from their expertise with the trust of *confianza*. In English, *confianza* translates literally as "confidence," but in practice *confianza* means a reciprocal relationship in which individuals feel cared for. *Confianza* is built through an ongoing, intentional process that is centered in local communities and involves mutual respect, critical reflection, caring, and group participation (Delgado Gaitan; Zentella). *Confianza* is also a trusting exchange of acceptance and confirmation between adult mentors and emergent bilingual students, and it has extraordinarily positive effects on the academic attitudes of youths, especially in language-minoritized communities.[2] I will expand on this notion of *confianza* and learning about students and their communities, as well as how openness to students' complete linguistic repertoires, in turn, affects their and their families' literacies and networks of bilingual support. I begin by asking these two questions: First, how can K–12 teachers emphasize more community connections in language arts pedagogy for emergent bilingual students? And second, why should language arts educators turn to community programs to develop bilingual learning programs? In the chapters that follow, I make specific suggestions for K–12 teachers about how to learn from the stories of emergent bilingual students in their communities as a means to help students become more confident readers, writers, speakers, and listeners. I recognize the challenges this task poses for teachers, knowing well that not all are fluently bilingual or have undergone formal professional development in teaching emergent bilingual students, and thus many may not feel adequately prepared to meet the needs of this growing demographic of linguistically diverse students.

Connections to the *NCTE Position Paper on the Role of English Teachers in Educating English Language Learners*

The Role of English Teachers in Educating English Language Learners serves as a starting point for some of this important work. One point in particular grounds the community work in which I am involved: learning from community funds of knowledge. Funds of knowledge are the "historically accumulated and culturally developed bodies of knowledge and skills essential for household or individual functioning and well-being" (González et al. 133). Funds of knowledge are bodies of local literacies, everyday knowledge learned through participation in home and community practices. Multilingual contexts become spaces to acknowledge, analyze, and engage community funds of knowledge that students bring to their language classrooms. *English Language Learners*, a policy research brief produced by NCTE, explicitly directs educators to locate community funds of knowledge: the "connections between academic content and [students'] funds of knowledge about home and community literacies can help students see these knowledges as resources for building academic literacy" (5). Those community connections are vital to the success of our emergent bilingual students and their families as they learn to navigate schools.

Why is it important for all teachers to build these relationships with communities? In part, it's because, while schools are powerful shapers of educational achievement and attainment, most of students' lives happen outside of schools—in homes, in neighborhoods, and among communities engaged with the activities of daily life—and for many of our students, in languages other than English. For students learning English, finding community becomes an important part of achieving a sense of belonging. The converse of belonging is feeling excluded, and schools should never be agents of exclusion. Inclusive community learning, I've found, helps teachers discover ways to design pedagogies that make productive use of both the literacy repertoires students bring to schools and the students' senses of community languages, identities, differences, and social justice. As Angie Zapata and Tasha Tropp Laman advise bilingual-responsive literacy educators, "we must welcome family and community members, lift their ways with words for children to appreciate, and elevate the dynamic ever-changing nature of languages as resources for writing" (376).

While the NCTE policy research brief establishes the basis on which educators can and must act, I believe we need even greater emphasis on collaboration and how we might best achieve it.

Educators who adopt a stance that builds on the strengths of communities must

1. meet communities on their terms—that is, educators learning from communities must be humbled and become students as they build commitment and trust with communities;

2. develop and extend neighborhood networks beyond schools, and adopt an orientation to assessment that applauds the critical, innovative, and creative abilities of bilingual individuals and communities; and

3. provide sustained volunteer service to communities as service learning and teacher training.

When educators become participants in bilingual communities, they partake in a form of community membership, demonstrating a kind of role-modeling that will both engage emergent bilingual youth and build *confianza* with communities—despite language differences. Dialogue also fosters *confianza* between community after-school programs and educators (Martínez et al.). *Confianza*, in other words, is feeling and knowing one is cared for. Angela Valenzuela argues that the "cared-for individual responds by demonstrating a willingness to reveal her/his essential self, the reciprocal relation" (21). *Confianza* truly creates not only a sense of validation and support but also a sense of trust, resulting in open discussions about schools and the community. Not surprisingly, establishing *confianza* takes time, but it is vital for opening channels for collaboration with community literacy research and after-school programs, especially those working with emergent bilingual students.

Why is this notion of *confianza* so vital for working with emergent bilingual students and their families? Research shows us the importance of *confianza* for bilingual Latin American and Latino/a students and their families, suggesting that sustained, dedicated commitment within nonfamilial groups of adults and youth positively affects the academic outcomes of children and adolescents in immigrant families (Louie; Monzó and Rueda; Smith). The narratives I collected from two after-school programs demonstrate the power of *confianza* as it links mentorship to schooling, especially for emergent bilingual students. The students involved in VBL and KUL come together through stories, and it is through these stories that the students make space to share their lived experiences. As collaborators connecting students, parents, and educators, the two after-school communities believe that emergent bilingual students can achieve higher educational goals with mentored, bicultural, and bilingual supports. These community partners inspire *confianza* through transformative visions for education and by building alliances among partners and activists.

In *Subtractive Schooling: U.S.-Mexican Youth and the Politics of Caring*, Angela Valenzuela argues that schools expect immigrant and minority students to give up—that is, "subtract"—their ethnic cultures and home languages, to erase these valuable supports for their educational development. Subtractive pedagogies, according to Valenzuela, "fracture students' cultural and ethnic identities, creating social, linguistic, and cultural divisions among students and between students and staff" (5). Through rigid standardization, subtractive schooling minoritizes the home cultures and languages students bring with them. By assessing the values of home language practices as "deficits," subtractive schooling disrupts relations within families, communities, and schools.

Subtractive schooling practices fail to recognize that emergent bilingual students come to schools with complex sets of histories, as members of diverse families and communities. Omitting these funds of knowledge from classrooms censors the lives of students from the curriculum. Regarding the alienating aspects of deficit perspectives, Kwangok Song writes, "Subtractive schooling approaches further create separation between school, home, and community, lessening the possibility of incorporating students' linguistic and cultural experiences into classroom practices" (342). To get to a place where multilingualism is valued, communities and educators need to move beyond language differences to build sustained trust across these differences, without fixating on supposed language barriers. In meeting the challenge of the NCTE policy brief, the instructors of today and tomorrow will become better acquainted with the everyday realities of bilingual families in monolingual-oriented K–12 schools. Supposed literacy "gaps" experienced by youth are often blamed on presumed deficits within the family and, by extension, the community. My fieldwork at KUL and VBL revealed something different, however. Rather than acting indifferently to education, communities of families and students were singularly preoccupied with overcoming linguistic obstacles. Indeed, some immigrant parents extended themselves in ways largely invisible to school authorities, because the social relations of *confianza* at these after-school community programs included these parents as stakeholders in the process. Of course, these parents were driven by fear of perpetuating economic hardship for

their children, but they were equally fearful of poor school performance perpetuating economic hardship. They exhibited remarkable agency in their willingness
to help their children, shuttling them from one after-school program to another
around different neighborhoods. Yet, too often, their children's schools kept
parents from exercising this agency. When students encountered language problems at school, their parents' fears that they might not complete school increased.
Building relationships with parents helps us realize the commitment they bring to
the table. Building relationships helps us reassess deficit theories that suggest what
parents cannot or do not do, replacing them with new beliefs that recognize the
assets and strengths these parents and families bring. Building relationships helps
us undertake pedagogies that draw upon the strengths of communities and their
unique language histories.

I want to share that I value what you do as teachers. As a university researcher, I fully respect the literacy learning happening in your classrooms and the
valuable impacts you make on the lives of your students. But in this book, I want to
encourage you to find educational spaces that exist outside of the classroom; these
are the spaces where I personally find special relevance as a student and a writer. I
trust in educators who want to learn, and I encourage us all to become students of
our students. They are the experts on their lived experiences among their communities beyond the classroom, and on how these communities reinforce much
of the work we do—although in different languages and using different ways with
literacy.

Teachers, with or without bilingual experience, who enter, meet, and establish rapport with their students' communities on their own terms will always learn
from them. I emphasize that pedagogies validate friendships forged *en confianza*
between current and future educators and communities. These relationships can
be articulated through writing that inquires into students' communities, their lived
experiences, and how they use all their languages. In this book, I will take you into
after-school programs that focus on these kinds of additive literacy approaches
while building *confianza* between adults and children. After-school mentorship
offers one way of realistically aligning parents' goals with those of children while
facilitating communication across generational, linguistic, and cultural differences.
As Guadalupe Valdés suggests in *Con Respeto: Bridging the Distances between Culturally Diverse Families and Schools*, programs for immigrant families "must be based
on an understanding, appreciation and respect for the internal dynamics of families
and for the legitimacy of their values and beliefs" (203). The two programs I profile
in this book demonstrate understanding, appreciation, and respect for family and
community dynamics, while also building on the sense of care that comes with
confianza.

Translingual Public Writing: Communities and Schools Recognizing the Dignity of Students' Languages

Our schools stress that speaking and learning in one language is the norm, and that any variation from that is considered nonstandard. In the United States—despite the wide variety of languages spoken—we subscribe to a monolingual language ideology that links English to citizenship and economic success. Indeed, bilingualism can be tolerated in addition to English, especially for students learning languages like Mandarin, French, Latin, Greek, or German, but English must be the dominant language of communication. There are "tracks" for emergent bilingual students, in particular a college track for students who hope to gain insight into another culture, and who perhaps may even study abroad to learn the language via international travel and tourism. And then there are forced bilinguals, also learning to be bilingual in context while gaining insight into another culture, but having their existing culture stripped away at the same time.

But that does not have to be the only way of thinking about language. What if we instead saw language through a pluralist ideology, a counterideology in which understanding multiple languages was the norm? That is the essence of research that argues for translingual practices of reading, writing, speaking, and listening as creatively complex tools, rather than obstacles to English language learning (Canagarajah, *Translingual Practice*; Horner et al.). Thinking of multilingualism as translingualism celebrates the innovative and creative abilities of individuals to move back and forth among a variety of language resources, including academic English.

Innovation and creativity are essential to teaching and learning English, and in the context of a translingual pedagogy grounded in the trust of *confianza*, they can be used to honor the literacy practices of local communities and communities' rights to their own languages. Literacy researchers and educators who make inquiries into students' communities can develop and mentor critical and creative community projects that respond to language, identity, and local issues of social justice, collecting and publishing local knowledge and histories. In the next chapters, I describe more of this connection between research and pedagogy, drawing on students' creative and critical composition of texts based on ethnographic research into their communities, as well as my own documentary writing. Such movements between classroom learning and community literacies engage all of us in dialogues that are creative, critical, and open to all genres and languages.

Narrating After-School Engagement in Emergent Bilingual Communities

Each chapter of this book contains narrative-driven explanations and vignettes from the VBL and KUL after-school programs. The chapters offer lesson ideas and links to NCTE materials and statements concerning emergent bilingual student success and community-school partnerships. The chapters weave together interviews, writing, artwork, and stories to reflect on the theme of creating a translingual language arts pedagogy that establishes *confianza* with students' communities. I draw lessons from local literacy- and ethnography-based assignments that bridge communities and schools.

Chapter 2 introduces VBL and KUL in further detail, while emphasizing the importance of *confianza* for ethnographic research with emergent bilingual communities. I also offer a brief overview of the history of Latin American migration to Kentucky and the state's growing emergent bilingual population. Chapter 3 presents a translingual framework for understanding students' linguistic repertoires and translanguaging practices to show how community programs help cultivate bilingualism through projects like the creation of a student writing anthology or the painting of a mural. Chapter 4 presents the voices of several VBL and KUL students, narrating how they built their own bilingual communities through shared stories and dialogues. Through their accounts of how they used photographs and fieldwork in their communities to compose translingual texts in multiple genres, they clearly express the concerns of bilingual students. Chapter 5 moves toward reassessing and countering ideologies of English Only immersion that subtract the bilingual gifts of students and their communities. In dialogue with communities, teachers can both build *confianza* and gain insight into local funds of knowledge to develop assessment strategies that value these bilingual gifts. Chapter 6 turns to the voices of three teachers in dialogue with KUL students, and shows how students' stories affected these teachers' approaches to community involvement. The three high school teachers gained the *confianza* of the KUL students, who composed writing for the student anthology that explored their bilingual histories, senses of social justice, and undivided support for KUL. Chapter 7 concludes this book with a call to organize community writing projects and language learning. The examples provided here offer teachers ideas for helping students compose creative and critical texts that are based on their lived experience and explore their communities. I note that *confianza* moves across languages but finds its home in the shared commitments of members in safe community spaces.

Building on the strengths of students and communities means connecting them with the considerable resources available to universities involved in literacy research, local outreach, multilingual teacher training, and student mentorship programs for future teachers. I call for community-school collaboration and expressive student literacy projects that treat the multilingual gifts of immigrant communities as sources of pride and identity. Students can be allowed to compose from their expertise as students—who spend many hours of their days learning to be students—in a school setting. But in after-school spaces, distant from the school context, they have the safety to critique schooling freely, opening windows into what schooling has been for them and what they envision it could be.

**Chapter
Two**

Emergent Bilingual Learning *en Confianza*

Students, volunteers, and staff at Valle del Bluegrass Library painted the mural pictured on the next page during the spring of 2012. A joint grant from a local arts-based nonprofit and the city's department of environmental quality funded the project. More than $5,000 in funding permitted the library to purchase materials and hire a local professional muralist who guided students in the construction of the piece, as well as to educate the community about the history of murals across Latin America and regionally in Kentucky. The project was not only an investment in arts and service learning, but also a public investment in the identity of this Kentucky *barrio*. Dozens of students of all ages, along with their parents, participated in the creation of the mural at various stages, taking field outings to study murals around the city, sketching ideas, organizing volunteers, and, finally, working with the artist to make the vision a physical reality. Students gave frequent input to ensure that the mural would encompass the theme of Kentucky's beauty and its rich agricultural history—including the laborers who work the land. The intention of the mural was to bring students together with local artists to personalize the library and send a message of *confianza* to the community, from the community. The public placement of the mural by VBL was a gift to the local community but was also strategic. The wall faces an intersection on a road that leads to the airport. Thousands of people see the mural each year. Indeed, the general reaction from locals was a pleasant mixture of pride and awareness of the changing nature and growth of the library. The liveliness of activity in the interior of VBL began to move outward, beyond the building's walls, to a dialogue with the public.

The outline of the state of Kentucky reflected the local landscape in the mural, but there was deeper symbolism, including explicit references to the horsing and farming industries and subtle yet important references to the immigrants whose work produced such a bountiful landscape, with purple figures in the shadows laboring among crops in the field. VBL's mural humanized the story of the community—the entire local community—and the valuable contributions of immigrants to the state's agricultural wealth. The mural also symbolized how VBL was an example of a community literacy space building identity and *confianza* in the service of education and learning about education, and proudly telling the story of local immigrant contributions to the wealth and beauty of the larger community.

Welcoming sites of community learning like VBL and KUL enable bilingualism and cultivate translanguaging practices that serve as creative and critical resources for students. The storytelling mode of mural art is powerful, but equally so is the attention to visual expression by students learning English and becoming bilingual. Both VBL and KUL are located in the middle of one of the largest communities of Spanish speakers in Kentucky, and because of this they have become important bilingual educational sites. Both bilingual programs are distinct from

Community collaborative mural on an exterior wall of Valle del Bluegrass Library.

local public schools and operate as community learning partnerships for publicly promoting and reclaiming home languages. This community model of schooling emphasizes education as a response to the immediate needs of a local bilingual constituency. For teachers, not only is this important to consider in terms of bilingualism and identity, but such expressive forms of writing also become ways for educators to create multimodal assignments that engage *confianza* to communicate to audiences.

In this chapter, I introduce the communities and contexts of VBL and KUL as they were situated in Kentucky at the time of my research. I imagine that similar programs exist where you live, although you may not know about them. Let me assure you that communities like these two can be found across the country. As resilient language-minoritized communities organize their collective resources, they locate spaces where their emergent bilingual practices find value, and where their confident voices count.

As I share more about these issues of *confianza* and bilingual community literacies, I provide narrative illustrations from KUL and VBL. I demonstrate how these communities offer spaces for learning outside of schools, spaces that encourage teachers to challenge their assumptions about their students and their communities, and to build relationships to sustain trust *en confianza*. Most important, though, I share how my research has taught me to be a better teacher, to learn how to know communities, and to teach future educators how to both research and learn from our students and their stories, struggles, hopes, and opportunities.

I end the chapter with an argument in favor of ethnographic methods for teachers and students in literacy classes at all levels. As I highlight with KUL and VBL, uncovering students' knowledge of themselves through stories is vital. The same, of course, goes for educators who learn about themselves by learning from the stories of their students and their communities. Such understanding influences their curriculum and expands *confianza*. But before I delve further into how you can build *confianza* with bilingual communities in your area, allow me to introduce you to VBL, KUL, and the context of Kentucky.

Valle del Bluegrass Library

Valle del Bluegrass Library has offered free after-school homework tutoring for emergent bilingual youths for over a decade. Located in a *barrio* in a small city in central Kentucky, VBL has mediated between the newly growing Latin American immigrant community in the area and local institutions, primarily local schools. VBL is the only bilingual public library in the state, and also the only one to offer after-school homework assistance for youth from kindergarten through twelfth grade—thanks, in part, to volunteer tutors and assistance from library staff. VBL also offers other programs and events geared toward preK, high school, and adult audiences.

The well-maintained library has ample lighting and windows. VBL is also equipped with computers, an abundance of resources in multiple languages, and several rooms to accommodate events and patrons. Of the six community branches of the public library system in the city, the 10,000-square-foot VBL is the newest. It was initially opened in 2004 and later expanded in 2008. A cooperative venture by the public library system, a large corporate bank, and multiple community partners, VBL found its home in a local shopping center on the west side of the city. Over the years, VBL has accumulated a vast collection of Spanish-language materials and has also expanded to occupy two-thirds of the west wing of the shopping center. The space has increasingly lent legitimacy to the emerging immigrant community living in the *barrio*. VBL is alive with bilingual activity and, during certain hours and days of the week, it's hardly a quiet place to do silent reading; during the school day, however, it quiets down. The homework program operates four days a week for four hours each session, and reaches thousands of students at all levels, but mostly those of elementary age.

According to US census data, the Latin American–origin population of Kentucky nearly tripled between 1990 and 2010, with nearly 90 percent of Latin American migration in Kentucky coming from Mexico (Marrow; Rich and Miranda). Brian L. Rich and Marta Miranda explain that the rapid growth of the Latino/a population in central Kentucky began when a predominantly male Mexican population engaged in more permanent low-wage jobs—as opposed to seasonal agricultural work (187). After 9/11, increased border militarization led to less seasonal migration, and a group of men who had formerly traveled back and forth between the United States and Mexico for work during different times of the year became a growing population establishing families with children in the United States. The heightened levels of border security compelled migrants to settle in Kentucky rather than leave and risk the inability to return.

Over the course of a generation, community programs appeared in Kentucky to help migrants adjust to life in the United States and find English-language support. The bilingual VBL has been a community safe space of civic engagement, offering not only support, but also advocacy, mentorship, and networking for the local Latin American immigrant community. As in many cities throughout the nation, the rapid emergence of a multiethnic community, spurred by transnational migration, has reshaped the local practices of communities that have responded— sometimes unwillingly—to multilingual needs.

Kentucky's history of responding to immigration has demonstrated a willingness among leaders of influence to move forward proactively as opposed to reactively. Many Latino/a-focused, community-based organizations have been

Bilingual signs for homework help at Valle del Bluegrass Library.

created to address the growing needs of the community. Though these programs have made progress to empower the community, the majority of them have been unsustainable. The lack of plans for sustainability and growth has resulted in great work starting but never reaching full fruition due to leader burnout and inadequate resources. VBL, however, has sustained itself for over a decade and has proved itself as a leading organization serving the interests and needs of the growing Latino/a population, principally because of its leadership, but also because of local government support. Without a doubt, the fiscal support and VBL's location in the heart of the *barrio* have created a space for literacy that the local community has grown and sustained.

Valle del Bluegrass Library has embraced its identity as a community learning center that provides academic enrichment opportunities during nonschool hours for children, particularly students who attend high-poverty and low-performing schools. VBL offers a broad array of enrichment activities that complement students' regular academic programs, as well as literacy and other educational services for the families of participating children. VBL's community programs include homework help for students in grades K–12, parental assistance with K–12 school enrollment forms, summer reading and academic enrichment programs, classes in English as a second language, and bilingual assistance for families. With the help of a generous community learning center grant, VBL has invited students into the program design process with a focus on developing leadership and supporting academic preparation. College awareness, preparation, and completion are now explicit values, talking points, and goals for all youth programs. VBL also has established a Teen Advisory Board that has collaborated in developing library programming and teaching leadership and facilitation skills, and whose members serve as community ambassadors providing outreach (including the mural project mentioned at the beginning of this chapter) and traveling tutor groups to neighboring schools.

From the perspective of a parent whose daughter benefited from VBL, thirty-five-year-old Berta, originally from Guerrero, Mexico, articulated the meaningful impact the library's programs had on her daughter, sixteen-year-old Celia, who was born in Kentucky. Berta found participation in programs at VBL to be important for Celia's academic support and for learning more about her identity. For a high school English writing assignment about genealogy, Celia interviewed her mother as a reporter learning more about Berta's life. Celia conducted the interview, transcribed it in Spanish, and translated the transcription into English before writing the version she submitted for class:

> I have witnessed that my child has developed in her maturity. She is proud to be Mexican American and celebrates both parts of her culture. She is starting to know who she is as a woman and what she is capable of doing as a person and in this world. She is outspoken, personable, smart, and determined to succeed.
>
> She grew up in a single parent home with a brother and a sister that went to programs at VBL to help her with school because I could not, because I don't know enough English. VBL also helped me to learn from people who speak Spanish. Now my daughter's looking to follow the footsteps of my two other kids and focus on her future. I want my family to be on the right track to get a great education and make something out of themselves. As a single mother and someone who did not get to go to college, I am so happy for my children to be in this position to make their dreams come true, and also for the help we found at VBL.

Her daughter's participation in VBL programs helped Berta learn more about educational opportunities that might not have been available to her otherwise because of what she viewed as English limitations. Despite these self-identified limitations, Berta found a bilingual community at the library to address the educational concerns she had for her children, which she was not able to do through the schools. Berta noted that VBL not only provided homework help, but also helped Celia to think about her identity and find a group of students who shared similar ambitions and constraints, thereby expanding her network with mentors and peers to help guide her toward college. Celia did graduate from high school a few years later, and she became the first in her family to attend college. Celia also became involved in a program at her college that found Latina mentors for elementary and middle school students. Several of these college mentors had attended VBL as children and returned to the library to serve as volunteers, and some as part-time employees.

Kentucky United Latinos

While it is undeniable that Kentucky's relationship with its growing Latino/a community has transformed meaningfully in the decade since VBL opened its doors, and that in many ways it has produced stronger and more progressive government and private recognition for this new ethnic population, it is important to note that this investment has also produced student leaders like those at KUL, who desire to be positive influences in their communities.

The Kentucky United Latinos after-school club formed in 2011 at a high school not too far from the *barrio* where VBL is located. In fact, KUL often meets at VBL since many of its students live within walking distance of the library. Most of the KUL students have VBL library cards and participated in the library's programs when they were younger.

The KUL club was originally a spinoff of the student technology leadership program at the high school. The high school, diverse by Kentucky standards, enrolls over 2,000 students; approximately 58 percent identify as White, 16 percent African American, 15 percent Latino/a, and 9 percent Asian. At one time, the school's technology leadership program offered after-school educational activities for students, and several students who would eventually form KUL met during these activities. Because of the strong Latino/a presence in the technology leadership program and the sense of solidarity among a bilingual group of friends, a community developed. When the program ended, students remained in contact and continued to meet in the school library after school. Eventually, the meetings attracted some two dozen students, including newcomer immigrant students learning English. Ms. Mason, a social studies teacher to several of the students, became involved and shortly thereafter offered her classroom as a meeting space. With Ms. Mason as a willing faculty sponsor, the Kentucky United Latinos club formed.

For students, the club is great for bilingual networking and finding out about college scholarships and other opportunities beyond high school. Responding to the need for information available in Spanish, KUL has produced a monthly newsletter and managed a school webpage with information for the community. With the coordinating

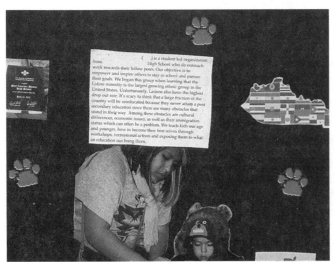

Kentucky United Latinos student presentation about community service and the importance of mentorship, and close-up view of the poster.

assistance of teachers, KUL has also partnered with a middle school to sponsor a student mentorship program. KUL members meet with middle school students to provide advice and guidance in English and Spanish to Latino/a students destined for their high school. As mentors, they also encourage the students to get involved in middle school activities and seek out ways to volunteer in their communities. Many KUL members have noted the importance of making a strong academic start as ninth graders, and how their community service has prepared them for college and future internships.

As previously discussed with regard to VBL, the city government has recognized and accommodated its growing immigrant community, funding initiatives in response to the advocacy work of local community organizers. KUL students have benefited from this advocacy work, receiving valuable mentorship and assistance, such as in the planning and painting of the mural discussed at the beginning of this chapter. To the benefit of the larger community, KUL students have felt compelled to give back and be of service. Eighteen-year-old Linda, a recent high school graduate and first-year college student, and the first in her family to attend college, described her experience with KUL. Linda had benefited from VBL's programs when she was younger, but in high school, she found they were geared more toward elementary and middle school students, and she turned toward her social network of friends instead. Through KUL, however, Linda has again been able to share positive views toward schooling with peers:

> KUL has helped me a lot through my last two years of high school. I used to not care about school much. Hanging out with my friends was more important to me than studying when I started high school. I regret it now, but at that age, nothing matters more than friends—and the friends I had didn't take academics seriously. I went to KUL, and I met great people and saw what they were doing was something different. *¡Y en español!* [And in Spanish!] It was a way to make new friends, Latino students who all wanted to go to college and talk about it in Spanish. I started to learn a lot about Latinos and what we could achieve. I liked using Spanish to learn more about this stuff.

For Linda, KUL became a learning community that demonstrated care, and where she felt invested in being a member. As she formed new friendships in the KUL community, Linda found that these peers accepted her pursuit of academic success, and that speaking Spanish with them brought her a new sense of closeness. As Linda grew as a student, she also continued to explore her Latino/a community and its contributions to city, state, and nation. Being surrounded by motivated bilingual KUL students enabled Linda to associate her bilingualism with academic achievement.

When Linda graduated high school and began to attend a community college, she became a member of a student organization serving diverse students. Several other KUL students who had graduated high school and moved on to colleges across the country also became members of similar organizations.

Learning Community Literacies by Practicing Ethnography

In *Writing Instruction in the Culturally Relevant Classroom*, Maisha T. Winn and Latrise P. Johnson build on the literacy research of Valerie Kinloch, offering ideas about students becoming ethnographers: Ethnographers conduct research in communities, paying close attention to the lived experiences of communities. Ethnographers use research methods such as observations, surveys, interviews, and photography to piece together cultural puzzles. Winn and Johnson write, "Students can be involved in participatory action projects such as examining 'spatial location and demographic trends' in their community . . . and study[ing] the linguistic practices of others through close listening" (71). Creative writing genres such as memoirs, poetry, and fiction can also become expressive outlets, especially when students research, listen, and learn with and from their communities. This kind of work leads students to share their research about local demographics and represent the voices of communities, in particular multilingual communities. The ethnographer-educator, as defined by Winn and Johnson, mediates between community audiences and participants, between representations and stories with subjective experiences, while being attuned to the voices of students navigating different genres. To this description of student ethnography, I add the importance of the ethical responsibility to be truthful while building *confianza*, both with the communities and with one's readership or audience.

This ethnographic approach fits perfectly with a translingual pedagogy in which students as researchers pose arguments about themselves as emergent bilingual learners, their intentions for their research, and their research questions. As a methodology, this kind of ethnographic approach involves a great deal of informal student writing, such as taking field notes, as well as reviewing and organizing data. It also contributes to emergent bilingual students' increasing awareness of social and cultural contexts, and works to build confidence, voice, and valuable research experience. This requires listening, sharing stories, and time—lots of time.

As an ethnographic researcher, I too have listened hard to the stories of the students, families, and teachers associated with KUL and VBL—research you'll see reflected in the pages that follow, which narrate the experiences of building relationships across languages. In order to gain this social connection, I've had to remove myself from my academic "ivory tower" and actively find ways to participate in a community largely forgotten by the institutional powers historically represented by the university. As an ethnographer-educator, I'm well aware that participating with the community under study necessitates a study of myself, of my position as a researcher, and of the possibilities of approaching a community's daily routines without obstructing them. Learning from communities also requires building rapport, which means spending time in the communities, volunteering, and getting to know people. For researchers like me and for educators—whether college level or K–12—this becomes a foundation for a critical pedagogy that respects the histories and experiences of communities as the basis for critiquing social and linguistic inequalities.

Django Paris envisions a "pedagogy of pluralism," where teacher knowledge and curriculum development include background research into how multiethnic spaces help youths navigate linguistic differences. In order to nurture this knowledge, Paris argues that "pre-service and practicing teachers must not only take courses on language, literacy and difference, they must also engage in critical ethnographic and sociolinguistic inquiry with the young people in their classrooms"

Educators Developing *Confianza* in Emergent Bilingual Communities

There are a number of ways K–12 educators can develop community ties, both within classrooms and in bilingual after-school spaces. The following ideas are ways to begin establishing trust between schools, communities, and students—though it's important to keep in mind that building community takes time and care, and can happen in many ways.

Out of class

- Volunteering as a mentor in established community spaces

- Developing a new community space within your school

- Partnering with existing groups that work with emergent bilingual students

- Creating after-school experiences for students and their parents

In class

- Inviting bilingual individuals to class as guest speakers

- Incorporating bilingual materials and inviting student interpretations and translations

- Crafting assignments that offer opportunities for students to bring in family home languages and community backgrounds

- Seeking out ways to challenge students' bilingual abilities, keeping in mind that bilinguals are not two monolinguals in one brain, but individuals with repertoires that extend beyond and between languages

(167). I also recommend that future and current literacy teachers get hands-on practice interacting with and learning about communities, especially in community programs that serve emergent bilingual students outside of school hours or during summer vacation months. All practicing teachers can learn, through community participation, about the funds of knowledge of students and their communities. This learning can help them develop classroom practices that embrace and care for students' strengths.

With this depth of experience with their students' communities, future and current literacy instructors grow as educators, developing pedagogy from practice. The challenge of honoring diversity in classrooms is a worthy one, and one we owe to our growth as educators, especially when learning and building a teaching philosophy as a student teacher, or developing additional practices as a seasoned teacher. Within this pedagogy of pluralism, we might send our students into the field to collect data to write about; to make inquiries into their own communities; to learn from the practices of the places they belong; or even to find out where they belong and uncover the meaning hidden there.

Lessons from Bilingual Community Literacy Programs: Translanguaging *Confianza*

Chapter Three

Most of the Kentucky United Latinos students initially met in elementary or middle school, where they were designated as English language learners or sometimes "limited English proficient," a label used by the US Department of Education that identifies these students as "other," assuming a monolingual proficiency in English as the norm and bilingualism as problematic. In these students' English as a second language courses, the KUL community began to form as they extended their interactions beyond class time, welcoming immigrant youth into this student-led, after-school initiative. I learned about the KUL students from one of their faculty advisors, Ms. Mason, a social studies teacher at the high school. Ms. Mason invited me to speak with the KUL students since I identified as both Latino and a first-generation college student. She was eager for me to talk with the students about college, and I was eager to meet them since I was new to the area. After the first meeting, I became a regular and, with the consent of KUL members and faculty sponsors at the high school, I began returning regularly to conduct writing workshops with the group.

The workshop sessions were held in the library after school on Wednesdays, and sometimes during organized events at VBL on weekends or weekday evenings. Most of the KUL students came from the same "feeder" elementary school, which had a 70 percent Latino/a population, and where nearly 50 percent of the total student body was classified as English language learners. Most of the students in the workshop lived in the *barrio* where VBL was located.

On one particular day, sixteen students showed up to the workshop. I brought notebooks for the students, and we began with timed freewriting. First, I asked the students to open to the first spread in their notebooks, and on the left page to write "Educational Stereotypes." Below this, students drafted a list of Latino/a educational stereotypes, ranging from "lazy," "ESL," "bad students," "troublemakers," and the like to some "sort of positive" descriptions such as "hard workers," "loyal," and "all about family." We began with these stereotypes, I told them, to determine what we were up against as Latinos/as and as a starting point for writing about our identities and the conflicts between who we are, who others expect us to be, and who others think we are as Latinos/as. Drawing on several items from the list, I asked students to talk about these perceptions and how they connected to bilingualism—the obvious missing stereotype!

Ms. Brice, one of the club sponsors and a Spanish and ESL instructor, looked on attentively, nodding as we talked. As the students moved on to a timed, focused freewrite on the subject of bilingual stereotypes, I noticed a new face. Fifteen-year-old Alberto had only recently arrived from Honduras. Alberto was in Ms. Brice's ESL class, and she brought him to the meeting to help him network with students who spoke Spanish. I noticed that Alberto looked anxious during this second freewrite. As the students worked, I walked over to him, kneeling to make level eye contact, and asked, "*¿hablas inglés?*" [Do you speak English?]

He said, "*No, casi nada*" [No, hardly at all].

"*Bueno,*" I said, "*está bien para escribir en español, pues* [that's good for writing in Spanish, then], or Spanglish if you want." I explained the instructions for the exercise using the word *estereotipos*. I took a chance with this word for *stereotypes*, using the English cognate because I was not sure the word existed in Spanish. I added the illustration, "*por ejemplo, en general la mayoría de la gente piensan que los hispanos son . . . ¿que?*" [for example, in general, most people think Hispanics are . . . what?]. Julia, a student sitting nearby, further clarified with an example from her notebook. Alberto nodded, and I pointed to my watch and tapped his notebook.

"Okay," he said.

As I stood, I assured all the KUL students that during freewriting, we welcomed Spanish and Spanglish. Alberto smiled when I said this to him, as did another student sitting near him who also appeared not to be completely confident with her English. I wondered what high school was like for Alberto and for her, and what expectations these two students had for themselves, their families, and their communities.

After several minutes, we regrouped to discuss some of the stereotypes students had written about. I was to learn that several students wrote in English and Spanish, but that the students spoke the most Spanish in response to listening to one another's writing. As they explored the negative stereotypes, I noticed the discussion growing active and even heated. I stepped out completely and allowed students to speak to one another. When they deferred to my expertise, I turned the conversation back to them and their expertise, responding to questions with questions rather than answers. At one point, a student named Valeria turned the conversation in an interesting direction.

"I have a stereotype about parents," she said.

Seventeen-year-old Valeria was KUL's elected president. She was born in Mexico but grew up in the United States. Scholars describe students like Valeria as generation 1.5 immigrants, people born in another nation who migrated when young and were raised and educated in the United States.

The stereotype, Valeria explained, was that "immigrant parents don't care about their kids in school." I braced myself for what she was going to say.

"So, like, my mom didn't graduate high school," she said. "She doesn't know how hard it is to go to college, but she tells me to go."

In Valeria's description, I instantly recognized the hallmarks of the immigrant bargain I had learned about in my research with immigrant community programs in New York City (Alvarez, "Brokering," "Translanguaging"). Children in immigrant families often face the predicament of dealing with parental pressures to become educated and succeed, despite what they see as their parents' "lack" of education. The immigrant bargain can leave young people with a feeling of generational disconnection in some cases. In others, the immigrant bargain reminds young people of the sacrifices their parents made for better lives.

I asked Valeria where this stereotype came from.

"Well, the parents don't speak English, so they don't help with school—*los padres no hablan inglés—*"

"And they are too busy working!" interrupted sixteen-year-old Ricardo, a fellow KUL member.

"They work too much, *ya están trabajando siempre, todos los días*, like third shifts and stuff. So they don't have time because they hardly ever see their kids," said seventeen-year-old Raquel.

"And they don't check the kids' homework," Valeria said.

I had to break into the conversation, first to request translations for students who needed help understanding what had been said. I then challenged the stereotypes about parents by mentioning to the KUL members that I had been to the *barrio*'s homework help tutoring program at VBL on the previous few evenings and had seen many interested parents there. They might not have spoken English, but they were invested in their children. And when they worked third shifts, they did that to help support their kids, not so they could avoid them. I had to stick up for parents, especially when their children misinterpreted signs they saw as fitting the negative stereotypes of their parents or the "deficits" schools ascribed to them. I also understood that while one half of the immigrant bargain was the pressure on children to succeed, the most powerful half was the parental sacrifice and sense of care that could be too easily overlooked, especially by teens.

Valeria considered my argument. She agreed and added, "Yeah, the library's a good place for the parents that go, but still, not all parents can go there. And it's hard for those neighborhoods that don't have a library like that, where parents and kids can get help with English and school."

"And some teachers don't know about places like the library either," Ricardo added. I agreed with Valeria and Ricardo. Several KUL students nodded and whispered to one another. Following this discussion, as a group we decided to do focused writing about parents and their challenges in helping children with homework. Some of the writing during this session we included in the book KUL members published, which I describe later.

How can educators best respond to the needs of students like Valeria, emergent bilingual students like her fellow KUL members, and communities across the nation seeking to partner with schools to empower students, families, and neighborhoods with effective educational practices and relationships?

The KUL students may be like some you know, students who did not learn English as their home language and who often speak to their parents in languages other than English. And maybe you are already aware of some of the complexities they face in living up to their end of the immigrant bargain. Maybe you are also aware of the stereotypes about bilingual students in your classroom, and stereotypes about their parents. As you know, these stereotypes are not the students *you* know. Faceless stereotypes are not human representations. The human representations we craft ourselves based on real-life interactions and relationships can disrupt the negativity associated with immigrant and bilingual communities. Indeed, these KUL students were quite aware of how stereotypes portrayed their families, home languages, and communities. Discussion of such stereotypes can challenge educators to rethink assumptions about bilingual education, bilingualism, and learning to read, write, and speak English. Conversations like these can help K–12 English language arts teachers expand their knowledge of the literacy practices of emergent bilingual students by engaging with them and their ideas in meaningful ways.

As NCTE's *English Language Learners* policy research brief rightly points out, teachers must be attentive to the ways emergent bilingual students "make connections between academic content and their own funds of knowledge about home and community literacies" (5). Awareness of these links, according to the brief, "can help students see their lived experiences as resources for building academic literacy" (5). To forge these connections using a translingual literacy pedagogy, educators must first participate in the lives of English learners in order to see what these funds of knowledge look like.

In this chapter, I examine the connections between pedagogy and *confianza* that I introduced in the previous chapters, and how VBL and KUL enact that trust. First, I explore a translanguaging perspective that recognizes and makes use of students' full range of linguistic abilities. Translanguaging practices enhance the feeling of *confianza* among members of the VBL and KUL communities. To illustrate this, I profile Ms. Clara, the branch manager of VBL, who epitomized *confianza* with the local immigrant community by honoring home languages and family struggles. I then describe how the creation of a KUL student writing anthology helped build partnerships, open up dialogues, and establish trust. I end the chapter with ideas for teachers to build on these experiences with after-school programs in order to challenge negative stereotypes about bilingual communities. The chapter also includes materials to help teachers plan writing assignments and exercises that involve translanguaging, and specifically digital platforms for creating and self-publishing community writing anthologies that embrace bilingual students' abilities, aspirations, imaginations, and social consciousness. The teaching approach I outline here develops from participation in the larger community, a literacy pedagogy that deepens the links between communities and classrooms.

Translanguaging in Literacy Assignments

These suggestions for long-term, formative projects encourage emergent bilingual students to write about their communities, celebrating diverse backgrounds, national origins, migration histories, cultural values, and home language practices.

- Involve students and their communities in discussions about the dignity of all languages as it relates to social justice.

- Focus on translanguaging practices during your interactions with students to help them represent and reinforce bilingualism in their writing.

- Create assignments that explore argumentation, narration, dialogue, timelines, and bilingualism.

- Incorporate visual texts, interview transcripts, oral histories, and freewriting as scaffolds for writing assignments.

- Urge students to write narratives that include characters speaking different languages, along with annotated English translations.

- Encourage students to transfer their knowledge from previous narratives and experiences to their writing.

- Challenge students to become learners who solve problems through stories while receiving feedback throughout the learning experience.

Linguistic Repertoires and Translanguaging Practices

A bilingual person is not like two monolinguals in one brain; in reality, bilingualism is much more complex, and bilingual competency should never be measured as two separate proficiencies. This is the central premise of the theory of translanguaging. Researchers use the term *translanguaging* to describe a repertoire of practices that creatively and critically make meaning beyond and between languages (García and Li Wei). Translanguaging is the movement back and forth between languages that occurs in bilingual communities. In practical terms, translanguaging describes students' movement across languages—for example, speaking and composing in Spanish and English within the same oral or written text, demonstrating comfort with both languages.

Linguistic repertoires are holistic and counter the terms of any debates about ELL "gaps" or "deficits." When we are open to translanguaging, we encourage bilingual practices and demonstrate our interest and trust in students as both learners and teachers, building *confianza* between students and teachers and between families and institutions. Establishing this level of trust can have extraordinarily positive effects on the attitudes of emergent bilingual students toward schooling, as they connect academic literacy with their own linguistic repertoires and come to see it as another language to incorporate into their speech and writing. The theory of translanguaging recognizes the fluid ways in which emergent bilinguals use language to make sense of the variety of situations and audiences they encounter.

Even in their English language arts homework, emergent bilingual students make strategic choices, selecting from their repertoire of translanguaging practices to critically and creatively navigate language differences. In "Negotiating Translingual Literacy: An Enactment," A. Suresh Canagarajah describes "envoicing strategy" as a tactical "consideration of voice that motivates writers to decide the extent and nature of code-meshing" (43). Envoicing strategies are the translanguaging practices of writers who draw on their linguistic repertoires to evoke voice and meaning as they create texts. For example, a bilingual student, when confronted with a writing assignment about a writer's voice, will consider how to represent speakers of different languages and how to address readers across languages. Educators who embrace students' linguistic repertoires as resources make the value of translanguaging explicit in their teaching and learning, rather than prizing only their students' supposed English fluency and thus treating home languages as obstacles to learning.

Here's a small but telling example from VBL: Notice in the top photograph on the next page how all the texts—both those written in English and those written in Spanish—are shelved together rather than segregated by language, including language reference books. This bilingual space, like the bilingual brain, is not divided into two neatly defined languages separated from one another, but rather reflects the mingled translanguaging practices of the community.

The sign in the photograph below demonstrates translanguaging as an everyday practice at VBL. The sign in the photo announced the afternoon and evening agenda for April 30, 2014, in both Spanish and English (notably in Spanish first, with English subtitles): the yearly *Día de los Libros* celebration, the regular nightly homework

Different language reference books shelved together at Valle del Bluegrass Library.

help, and a weekly course in the Japanese martial art of aikido. The *Día de los Libros* special event featured bilingual songs, as well as free books and school supplies for all children in attendance. The celebration was a social event in the community and one celebrated bilingually. More than 100 families were in attendance, which was not an unusual number for VBL during the school year.

The sign in the photograph shows how bilingual communities move strategically between languages in their daily practices, and suggests some important points about how to reach Latino/a (and other emerging bilingual) communities by building on the strengths of bilingualism as a way to bridge communication gaps between families and schools. Among the Spanish-speaking adult attendees of the *Día de los Libros* event, the majority were first-generation immigrants from Mexico. Child attendees were a combination of first- and second-generation Latino/a, African American, and White youth from the neighborhood, a historically racially mixed, low-income area. The younger children reflected the diversity of the neighborhood and the bilingual fluidity happening in their schools

Día de los Libros (Book Day) at Valle del Bluegrass Library.

and in Latino/a spaces in the *barrio*. Students identifying as Latino/a constituted 70 percent of the student body of 700 at the nearest local elementary school, White students composed 15 percent, and African American students 13 percent. Nearly 50 percent of the entire student body was classified as ELLs. Nearly 97 percent of all students at the school qualified for free and reduced lunch. For the community, poverty was an unfortunate equalizer, and public spaces like VBL both supplemented learning outside of schools and connected parents in shared circumstances. With events like *Día de los Libros*, VBL sought to meet community demand, while also being sensitive to the bilingualism and diversity of the neighborhood.

Indeed, most of the students and parents who attended that evening's event were emergent bilinguals, and Spanish was the home language for the majority of attendees. But it was the power and promise of academic English literacy that brought the community together in the public space of the library. Given the complex balance between the recognition of home languages and the value placed on English proficiency, English language arts educators must question their role in this power relationship: Do teachers—without meaning to—encourage students to misunderstand their linguistic repertoires? In schools' emphasis on a single variety of a language, do we create unintended consequences for our students and their parents?

Valle del Bluegrass Library not only allows but also encourages emerging bilingual parents to communicate their ideas and emotions to their children using all resources available. Lessons from the VBL and KUL after-school programs connect English-language mentors with bilingual and emerging bilingual students and, in so doing, help to counteract children's potentially negative attitudes about their literacies and encourage respect for home languages. Both programs are examples of local communities finding spaces where bilingualism can be nurtured outside of schools, and where emergent bilinguals can utilize their full linguistic repertoires. Whereas public and private schools are typically formal educational units organized around a standardized curriculum established and regulated by larger bureaucratic agencies, locally based programs like VBL and KUL are sites of community-building around schooling. In this community model, education rises from the immediate bilingual needs of a local constituency. The community builds trust collectively, but, as I demonstrate in the following section with the example of Ms. Clara at VBL, *confianza* develops on an individual, human level through the stories that members share.

Translanguaging in K–12 Language Arts Classes

Here are four pedagogical strategies educators can employ right away to build translanguaging into language arts courses. These methods are intended to encourage students to use their emergent bilingualism as an academic resource, and to increase family engagement in students' research projects in their communities.

1. Acknowledge the academic benefits of studying emergent bilingual students' autobiographies. Writing courses at all levels stand to gain by incorporating ethnography, and especially projects that take students into their communities to conduct field research as homework (like the interview assignment Celia conducted with her mother in Chapter 2). Students' interviews should be transcribed with attention to accents, and translations should be included when necessary. To provide further social perspectives, assign ethnographic homework projects in which groups of students of different backgrounds research and write about their classmates' homes and languages. These types of tasks require students to practice reflective, critical thinking, resulting in relevant language arts homework projects that are rooted in students' lived experiences.

2. Offer parents more detailed instructions or assistance guides for homework. This shows appreciation for parents' role in their children's educational trajectories and makes it easier for them to share information with mentors providing homework help. Likewise, more detailed teacher comments on report cards would also be beneficial, allowing emergent bilingual students and mentors to create plans of action for family involvement.

3. Ask students to gather field notes about the languages used in their homes and communities. This invites students to consult with diverse participants, including individuals who speak, read, and write different languages. Teams of students exploring the narratives and languages of their classmates will find they have much to offer as they share language differences in classroom community spaces. Students sharing fieldwork data in discussion workshops can demonstrate to fellow field-workers how bilingualism enhances language interpretation tactics.

4. Encourage bilingual participation by giving assignments that involve translation. Foreign-language videos or news clips that include English subtitles, for example, are excellent texts for analyzing and critiquing translations, as well as visualizing international locations, stories, or events. This can invite emergent bilinguals to share their expertise while also exposing students to the translanguaging practices of their classmates. Language arts educators can also invite students to interpret, translate, paraphrase, and code-switch during class, calling attention to language differences for discussion and analysis.

Ms. Clara, the Face of Community *Confianza*

Mentorship research (Hirsch et al.; Rhodes; Rhodes and Lowe; Smith; Suárez-Orozco et al.) argues that sustained, dedicated commitment between adults and youth outside of family groups has positive effects on the academic outcomes of children and adolescents in immigrant families. This is no surprise to scholars who have conducted long-term research with youth in the context of their communities, and who have developed relationships over time that are essential for both rapport and trust. Establishing rapport, like *confianza*, takes time, and it is an important way to open doors for community literacy research and after-school programs, especially those engaging with students outside academic contexts.

As literacy educators, we must strive to build *confianza* with communities over time in order to understand their views and ways of articulating thoughts and feelings. As a teacher, I listen, and as a community researcher, I work to participate and build trust. I am attuned to the literacy practices I learn about, and my closeness to my research indicates the depths of respect and direct contact I invest in the community's literacies, as well as the community's investment in me. But it has taken time for me to gain *confianza*, and it is a continual and transformative process. For you, too, it will take time. The rewards, however, are great. To give you a better idea of this process, let me introduce you to Ms. Clara, the branch manager of VBL and one of the many adults I've met across the nation who have earned the *confianza* of entire communities.

When I first arrived to meet with Ms. Clara to propose a research study, I was pleasantly surprised, because I found I had met her previously. Two days before, Ms. Clara had observed me tutoring some youths during VBL's after-school homework help program, and she had pulled me aside before I left to thank me for reading in Spanish and English with the children, as well as for the attention I'd given to each student—I had spent 45 minutes with each of the three tutees, helping with language arts, science, social studies, and math homework, using Spanish and English to communicate across all of these subjects. It was my first week tutoring at VBL. After conducting research at an after-school homework program in New York City for several years, I understood that homework help programs often were in need of qualified volunteers with teaching experience. I sought out homework programs in Kentucky and came upon VBL, where I decided I could make a difference and learn more about local immigrant communities.

"You must be a teacher," she'd said.

"You might say that. But adults, not kids," I'd said.

"Well, you have a way with kids, and we're glad you're here. *Gracias.*"

We had exchanged quick pleasantries, but not introductions. I'd had no idea the woman I was speaking to then was the branch manager. I had assumed she was a staff member or another volunteer, as I'd noticed her helping students with homework at another table. Looking back now, I'm thankful that the manager would take time out of her schedule to volunteer with homework help.

Ms. Clara welcomed me into her office. "*Bienvenido,*" she said.

As we walked into her office during the afternoon of our visit, I noticed a hanging Caribbean country-style house model on one wall, as well as two Huichol paintings on the opposing wall, in a style specific to the Tarascan indigenous people from the state of Michoacán in Mexico. This seemed significant to me, because I knew through interacting with folks around the community that Michoacán was one of the primary states of origin of immigrants in the region. Also on the wall were drawings made with crayons and markers of various figures with names below them on both lined and unlined paper, made by the youth of VBL and Ms. Clara's grandchildren.

Ms. Clara had been the manager at VBL since it opened its doors in 2004. I told her I had heard about her community leadership through my connections in K–12 schools in the area. Ms. Clara was very involved with local politics and also with helping area Latinos/as find educational, medical, and legal resources. In fact, as the library's primary public face, Ms. Clara was viewed as the kind of person who would help in whatever way she could. In an interview, she responded to the general view of the library as not just a library:

> A lot of people, when they visit us or when they learn about us, they say, "You're more like a community center." That, in and of itself, doesn't make the library any different from other libraries. Libraries have always been the center of a community, or a very important part. It's just that we do it a little differently. We'll go a step further. We don't want our patrons to feel like, the minute they've come in, they've just hit another wall. They hit so many walls in their everyday life.

Understanding the difficulties that this community faced on a daily basis—because of language, cultural, and/or immigration status barriers—demonstrated the library's support of bilingualism and biculturalism. It also demonstrated how VBL, as a safe space, did work that resembled what ethnographers do when they go out into the field and observe, listen, and try to understand a community's ways of knowing, as well as its needs. Yet, in VBL's case, the goal was to meet those needs as efficiently as possible. By offering bilingual texts and hiring bilingual staff, VBL not only attempted to meet the neighborhood's sociocultural and bilingual needs, but also nurtured the residents' emerging biculturalism. The bureaucracies and standardized ideologies of public schools often make it difficult for people in administrative positions to immediately respond to parents' and students' bicultural needs, but Ms. Clara was in a different position. Perhaps this was because her life experiences in many ways resembled those of the community she served. Ms. Clara was attuned to the strengths and challenges of the local Latino/a community. Her bilingualism also made her a point of contact for schools and parents.

Ms. Clara was born in Havana, Cuba, grew up in Florida, and had lived in Kentucky for over 20 years. She described how her family left Cuba as refugees when Fidel Castro came to power: "I'm an immigrant. Not like the situation of many of the families immigrating here now, but an immigrant. We were refugees, and in that sense, I share the same pattern of moving away and looking for a better life. That's not a crime—to want a better life."

The previous branch manager and Ms. Clara were both largely responsible for researching and applying for program funding. The social programming, such as homework help and teen reading programs, as well as computer and Internet access at VBL, were largely subsidized through federal grant initiatives aimed at preventing violence.

"That's how we started," Ms. Clara said. She continued:

> The idea was to use education as one means of reaching the community and to calm the violence. To give the kids something to do. We expanded over the years as more immigrants found us and discovered us as a safe place. We wouldn't deny them, and I think they felt that from other organizations. I know what these kids experience. I remember growing up, and how I started school and I didn't know the language.

Ms. Clara brokered this knowledge from her experience of growing up bilingual into how she approached her work as a translingual advocate for the community. She also pointed to the challenges faced by bilingual youth in helping their parents. I asked Ms. Clara about her memories of becoming bilingual in her family, and if she helped her parents learn English:

> I used to translate, and it was hard. Hard because some of the words were difficult, I didn't know what I was saying. Like with taxes! How is a kid supposed to translate that? And my parents would be so upset with me, and I would be upset with them. Yes, I think what you'll find are some similar stories, and I hope teachers and schools can help us to figure out how to take away some of that stress for these families, because they have so much already.

Curious, I asked Ms. Clara if she had ever been an educator.

"Yes," she answered. "For as long as I've been a librarian, I've been an educator. But I teach outside of schools, and the schools here need all the help they can get with serving the immigrant community."

Ms. Clara forcefully acknowledged the fundamental inequalities Latino/a students in Kentucky faced as they struggled to keep pace with their peers who grew up with more "advantages," as she put it. "I want these kids to have advantages because they don't have them. I know them, I know their families, I know what they are going through. I lived it."

I mentioned to Ms. Clara that I was surprised to see so much institutional support for Latino/a families in Kentucky. I explained my research in New York City, and how the families there had no such institutional support and had to quite literally "go underground"—in the basement of a church—to find the space they needed to organize their after-school program.

Ms. Clara nodded as I said all this, and answered:

> I'm not going to lie, it wasn't easy. There was some backlash from the community because of how we approached Spanish and English together. Not the entire community, but there were those parties who had a problem. But the overwhelming majority of the community supports what we do. We have a lot of support, through grants, but also politically, and as you see from the community. We are located in the heart of the *barrio*.

Whatever controversy had initially surrounded bilingualism at VBL had dissipated, as the library played a functional role in the community for building goodwill in a safe environment. The library's bilingualism also legitimized Spanish as a valuable language in the community, valued enough to warrant a public space, with staff that could support community literacies. This genuine sense of care was not unique to Ms. Clara, but her disposition certainly set the tone for the VBL staff, who approached the local Spanish-speaking community with dignity, seeking to create *confianza*. For instance, Ms. Clara shared hugs and laughs with patrons with whom she had established trust, and she always greeted new patrons literally with her arms open, and in both Spanish and English. She also set the tone for translanguaging practices to be embraced by all VBL members.

Ms. Clara was not like most librarians, and VBL was certainly not like most libraries. Ms. Clara's investment as a mentor at VBL made her a resource for the community. She had come to know many families in her years as a librarian-educator and community advocate. Entering communities is more than simply showing up for a few hours. Educators must connect to communities, as well; like Ms. Clara, they must be confident in the strengths of these communities, and also aware of the communities' linguistic struggles for equality and dignity. Community leaders like Ms. Clara are important people for all teachers to know. Building sustained trust lays the groundwork for literacy education that benefits communities through mentorship for writing, especially for young writers—a relationship that blurs the lines between teacher and student in the sense that both are committed to learning, growing, asking tough questions, and caring about each other. Successful students have advocates like Ms. Clara, but they also advocate for one another and for their communities.

Community programs can teach educators a great deal about what *confianza* looks like. The complex relationship of *confianza* requires educators to be guided by the dignity of their students' local lived experiences. Educators should be attuned to students' translanguaging practices, linguistic repertoires, and lived experiences through shared educational action and community literacy projects. What does it mean to guide students through community literacy projects? In the next section, I describe the example of a local publishing venture the KUL students and I undertook together. These students were in touch with their shared struggles and bilingualism as vehicles for expression, and their awareness of audience and community dialogue guided their translingual ways with words and attention to social justice. For this reason, KUL students created an anthology of documentary student writing to share their experiences, profess their community's strengths, and build connections between schools and community literacy learning projects.

Making Community Literacies: The KUL Writing Anthology

The KUL club presents an important lesson for teachers of writing, about how *confianza* and mentorship intersect in a translingual pedagogy outside of classrooms—and how these insights might be used within the school classroom, too. The KUL students self-published an edited anthology of their writing, and this volume became one way for students to free their bilingual voices from monolingual thinking. Nineteen KUL students wrote in various genres, using their full linguistic repertoires, exploring through their writing and dialogues the resilience of Kentucky's Latin American immigrant communities. The subjects the KUL members explored in the book came alive through the forms they chose to write in, and their movements across languages gave them permission to question the "norm" of academic English as they created texts from their lived experiences.

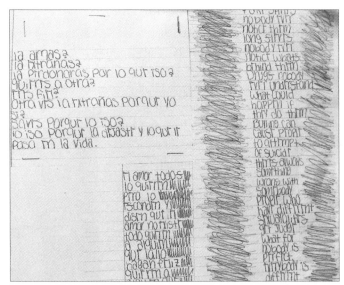

Initially, creating a book was not the goal of the KUL writing project. The project began as part of a series of informal writing workshops I led. Students enjoyed these workshops and continued to invite me to meetings. As interest grew, students brought up the idea of photocopying poems to distribute to the middle school students KUL mentored, as well as to students at different schools. With some discussion and online research, we discovered we could self-publish our own book

Rough draft of a poem by a Kentucky United Latinos student, shared during a workshop session.

through Amazon's CreateSpace, a user-friendly platform for book design and distribution. Students interested in publishing the book-length project contributed writing and artwork. They revised their work based on suggestions and comments from participants in our workshops, and also from me. Months later, after several writing workshops and drafts, these various texts became the final product. Students submitted poems, fiction, nonfiction, and artwork. KUL students also gave input and voted on the book's cover, title, and organization, in addition to reviewing proofs and making further revisions to their work.

The book was divided into connected sections that spoke to different themes chosen by the KUL students. The first section, "Communities/*Comunidades*," pointed to the importance of community for student involvement. The next section, "Families/*Familiares*," detailed the central role families played in the lives of the students. This was followed by "Goals/*Metas*," which offered a window into how these students envisioned their futures and the importance of education in pursuing their dreams. The last section, "Identities/*Identidades*," dealt with the divided sense of self that children of immigrants face as each generation comes to terms with multilingualism and biculturalism. These texts reflected the KUL students' perspectives on growing up Latino/a in the US South, as well as their bilingual voices.

The students also marketed this book to raise funds for scholarships for graduating KUL members. After some discussion, however, the KUL students agreed that, rather than awarding multiple scholarships, they should pool the money into one single scholarship to help one deserving student. They drew up the criteria for the scholarship, which included contributions to the book, a personal statement about community and KUL service, and an increasing GPA over the four years of high school (rather than cumulative GPA).

With the support of donors, KUL purchased copies to distribute to local K–12 schools, universities, public libraries, and after-school programs across the state. VBL also purchased a few dozen copies for its shelves. In the end, sales of the book produced a $2,000 scholarship for Linda, the KUL student previously mentioned in Chapter 2, who graduated and began attending a local community college. During a ceremony held at VBL, KUL students read their work from the book, and Linda and her family were presented with the scholarship. Many of the KUL students' parents and siblings attended, as well as students and teachers from the local high school, and members of the university community. Linda used the funds to pay tuition for her first year of community college and purchase books. Even after graduating from high school, she still attended KUL meetings.

The workshops I conducted with KUL students incorporated creative writing methods alongside text models from the US Latino/a literary canon, including such bilingual poems as "I Am Joaquín" by Rodolfo "Corky" Gonzales, "How to

Online Self-Publishing Platforms

The following online publishing venues feature different pros and cons. Though some cost money, others are free. All publish materials on demand as either digital or paper texts. Keep in mind that other forms of publishing are also available online, such as comic strips and videos. Also consider options available for tablets and other mobile devices, which might be more accessible for some. The best way to learn about these platforms is to experiment with them, as each is geared toward different uses and requires different levels of expertise.

- Amazon CreateSpace: www.createspace.com

- Bookbaby: www.bookbaby.com

- Kindle Direct Publishing: kdp.amazon.com

- Lulu: www.lulu.com

- Smashwords: www.smashwords.com

Tame a Wild Tongue" by Gloria Anzaldúa, "Legal Alien" by Pat Mora, and "To a Jornalero Cleaning Out My Neighbor's Garage" by Eduardo Corral. Noting how all these writers translanguaged encouraged the KUL writers to do the same, leading them to explore their cultural identities.

Mora's poem, for example, begins by translanguaging: "Bi-lingual, Bi-cultural / able to slip from 'How's life?' / to '*Me'stan volviendo loca*'" [they are driving me crazy]. The poem describes the "sliding back and forth" that emergent bilingual students experience as they move between contexts when writing in English and speaking in Spanish. Poems such as this encourage students to explore their lived bilingual experiences and to extend their communication practices across both English and Spanish in order to achieve the fullest expression of their voices, ideas, and identities—and free themselves from assumptions that judge their bilingualism in English Only terms.

These workshops were never called classes, no grades were given, and participation was voluntary, though all students who attended the sessions wrote and shared their work. The promise of publishing their work was the largest draw, in addition to the *confianza* shared by the KUL group through conversations and friendships. The KUL anthology became a collective portfolio of community writing and artwork.

Students shared their writing during workshops, which created opportunities for dialogue. These informative discussions helped me understand how the safe space of the KUL community allowed students to communicate honestly, without worrying about their English abilities, and welcomed the full potential of communication beyond language differences. Often these conversations went beyond meetings and into the Facebook group formed by KUL.

The students' writing also sparked discussion about families. During one writing challenge, they wrote their autobiographies in two paragraphs. They shared snapshots of their lives, where they came from, and their role models—either actual or those they foresaw themselves becoming. When the KUL students shared their finished stories, several cried. The experiences were emotionally charged for the readers and the audience, especially when they reflected on the sacrifices of parents. Nydia, an eleventh grader, spoke about both VBL and her classroom teachers as major influences. She thanked Ms. Brice, one of

KUL's faculty sponsors, as she wiped tears from her eyes. "I want to be like that, too, someday," Nydia said. "I want to be like you because you help so many of our *gente*." *Gente* translates to "people," and it was telling that she translanguaged when speaking of her community, in which she included Ms. Brice as a member. Ms. Brice gave Nydia a hug and thanked her for her kind words.

Building Bridges with Emergent Bilingual Communities

Communities of teachers and students who learn from one another can expand bilingual literacy repertoires even as they establish *confianza*. Those who work in community programs can learn from educators about assessment, how to arrange courses for different grade levels, and specific strategies for educational success in the current curriculum and in advancement to higher education. For educators, this contact will also influence course planning and literacy projects, such as the KUL student writing anthology.

Members of KUL who felt comfortable and confident in their abilities to express themselves found ways to represent their struggles in learning English to other students who shared similar experiences. These students, in turn, were able to learn from shared community narratives and perspectives. Such interactions decrease the focus on individual competition among students who feel like they fall outside the so-called "mainstream." According to Bob Fecho in *Writing in the Dialogical Classroom: Students and Teachers Responding to the Texts of Their Lives*, making dialogue a part of writing assignments "represents the intersection of academic and personal writing, allows for multiple voices and languages, [and] involves critical thought, reflection and engagement across time, while also creating opportunities for substantive and ongoing meaning making" (7). The creation of shared meanings in safe spaces is important for students learning English, helping them not only engage their bilingual community, but also learn how to keep a bit of distance from the pressures of schooling.

As daunting as all this community outreach sounds, busy educators can foster *confianza* with communities like VBL and KUL in a number of relevant ways to incorporate community literacy engagement into writing assignments. Encouraging translanguaging inside classrooms is the first step in recognizing students' full linguistic repertoires. As multilingualism and globalization continue to shape one another, all students will develop translingual skills. One way to approach this pedagogical opportunity is to affirm the positive attributes of children's translanguaging, as well as their emergent bilingualism, ultimately developing a greater appreciation for these skills in curricula by highlighting relevant moments in classroom discussions and texts. As the next chapter describes, students' creation of their own texts offers the greatest potential for engaging local audiences.

Helping students engage with their communities and publish for real-world audiences provides incentives for those often stereotyped as "too quiet" to make themselves heard. Students who are given opportunities to voice their views through writing speak with and on behalf of their communities from a position of knowledge and experience. In the next chapter, we hear more from the voices of emergent bilingual students as they share their stories beyond and between languages. This bilingual approach may be unpopular with English or Spanish purists, but the contexts and histories of bilingual individuals are not one or the other; they are both and more. The next chapter details more lessons reinforcing the importance of *confianza* when translanguaging in the field.

The Shared Commitments of Communities and Schools: The Voices of Emergent Bilingual Students

High school student Bianca, with collaboration from classmates in her ESL course at school, drew the artwork in the photograph on the following page, entitled *Don't Cry*. Bianca, a ninth grader, had migrated to Kentucky from Cuba earlier in the school year, and had been a member of KUL ever since. Ms. Brice, Bianca's teacher and one of KUL's faculty sponsors, had accompanied her to KUL's regular meeting the week after she arrived.

Though she had studied English in Cuba, Bianca felt more confident in Spanish, suspecting that her "lack" of English made people think less of her abilities as a student and artist. Bianca enjoyed Japanese manga graphic novels and anime films, and she found her voice in creating similar artwork. Her sketch was inspired by Japanese figure-drawing aesthetics and depicted the emotional frustrations she experienced as she learned English—the frustration of tears, the frown, the clenched hand in a defensive gesture, and the silence. Bianca's immediate audience became her newcomer classmates, and rather than sign the image herself and leave its disheartened figure silent, she asked her classmates to take part in her art. Bianca realized her classmates shared her frustrations in

Don't Cry by Kentucky United Latinos member Bianca.

becoming bilingual in a space where being a "native monolingual" was the price of fluency. She asked them to write "don't cry" in their home languages around the image. As you can see, twenty different languages surround the image, speaking simultaneously and with equal dignity, and thus contributing to the social significance of the artwork. Twenty different languages—in Kentucky, a state commonly imagined as homogeneously English monolingual. In fact, according to the local K–12 school district's data, 80 different home languages were reported among its students.

The deep emotional connections to language and diversity in *Don't Cry* remind us of the pains of becoming bilingual, shared by students from a variety of contexts. I think *Don't Cry* also reminds us that all the languages of our students are gifts, and those gifts shape their identities as unique individuals in communities that speak to one another across languages and differences. The language and literacy practices of emergent bilinguals like Bianca and her classmates, and bilingual communities like the schools and neighborhoods in which they live, show the potential of translingual pedagogies.

In language arts courses that embrace a translingual pedagogy, students' writing projects might focus on using multiple languages to both build critiques and compose expressive projects that reflect local, national, and global struggles and histories. This type of writing pedagogy means embracing lessons from literacy research on the practices of communities—especially in terms of immersing students in diverse activities, performances, and genres, across languages, generations, and social classes. Reading of the word in order to reread and rewrite the world offers the liberating potential to envision social justice across languages.

Naturally, schools and communities are settings where youth experience many stories. Both settings have the potential to be opportunities for student-centered research about learning. The struggles of emergent bilingual students, young people coming of age and fighting the battles that come with growing up, are important for educators and parents to listen to and learn from. This chapter offers a better understanding of projects that explore community from the perspectives of emergent bilingual students sharing their writing. I begin this chapter with examples of write-around exercises for emergent bilingual students that tap into the strengths of their communities. A collaborative poem by two KUL students provides an example of translingual verse that addresses social justice, and an illustration of how the sharing of writing developed *confianza* among students. Next, I turn to several examples of expressive writing and photography by VBL and KUL students. These students delved deeply into local funds of knowledge, all demonstrating critical awareness appropriate for academic inquiry. I end the chapter with another translingual poem from a KUL student that illustrates the resilience of bilingual communities in cultivating positive attitudes toward schooling while also coming together to critique English Only ideologies that categorize their bilingualism as a deficit (Martínez). These examples are intended to provide language arts educators with ideas for ways to engage parents and local communities in conversations about educational goals, motivations, and the expressive ways emergent bilingual students use reading and writing as they explore their linguistic repertoires.

Writing for Real Audiences, Sharing Stories, and Studying Stories

How can literacy educators help students realize the power of their linguistic repertoires? Angie Zapata and Tasha Tropp Laman argue that "a translingual approach to writing instruction . . . affords young bilingual writers opportunities to develop composing processes and texts that require creative and thoughtful movement between, across, and within their linguistic repertoire to communicate and transcend traditional monolingual writing processes" (367). Zapata and Tropp Laman's call for a translingual writing pedagogy resonates with my experience of developing collaborative literacy projects with emergent bilingual students. In *Becoming Writers in the Elementary Classroom*, Katie Van Sluys describes literacy projects in which students compose narratives exploring identity, language, social inequities, and social justice. One such project is a chain writing activity called a write-around, in which group members pose a question or begin with the first line of a composition, even a narrative. At timed intervals, students pass the page to the next person in the circle. As the cycle continues, each writer composes the next part of the text, answers a question, or continues the narrative (which might require a certain number of lines or sentences). This exercise requires sharing, and students who examine their own experiences learn from other students who are also delving into their experiences.

Van Sluys's write-around exercise could also provide freedom for emergent bilingual students to experiment with translanguaging, and to play with their full linguistic repertoires to articulate their experiences of learning English, challenging how institutions have shaped their views of their self-worth. With each interval, teachers could encourage emergent bilingual students to try expressing the text in different languages. If groups are large enough, the exchanges could continue for up to several pages in order to generate as much material as possible. Teachers can experiment with the durations of writing intervals and the number of switches between group members. (I also encourage teachers to participate in the activity in professional development sessions as a way of thinking through the challenges students face.)

What follows is a write-around cowritten by fifteen-year-old Ana and sixteen-year-old Ernesto that touches on lived experience, biography, becoming bilingual, and identity.

Ayer en la noche escribrí un poema,   [Last night I wrote a poem,]
y los Latinos eran el tema.   [and Latinos were the subject.]
Todos somos diferentes.   [We are all different.]
Dicen burros.   [Some call us unintelligent.]
Pero somos inteligentes.   [But we are intelligent.]
Picking, packing, and cleaning
seeing my parents struggle keeps me
          dreaming.
No me digas que no tengo la razón   [Don't tell me I'm not being reasonable]
porque todo lo que hago   [because everything I do]
lo hago con el corazón.   [I do with heart.]
I have a voice to make some noise and
that's my choice.
Aprendí de mis padres   [I learned from my parents]
a trabajar duro,   [to work hard,]
pero todo el racísmo   [but all the racism]
me hace sentir inseguro.   [makes me insecure.]
Sin embargo todavía sueño   [However, I still dream]
en un futuro.   [of a future.]
Hablo inglés y español,   [I speak English and Spanish,]
y soy Americano.   [and I am American.]
Las personas me miran   [People see me]
y me dice Mexicano.   [and tell me I'm Mexican.]
Feeling like I didn't have an opportunity
coming to this land gave me the agility
to do my best even though I have
          so much stress.
Overcoming my fear
makes me appreciate that I'm here.
Estando aquí y aprendido mucho   [Being here, I've learned so much]
y se que lo puedo lograr si lucho.   [and I know I can achieve success if I fight.]
Quiero dar gracias a todos ustedes   [I want to thank you all]
por hacer esto posible,   [for making this possible,]
por recordarme que en este país   [for reminding me that in this nation]
no soy invisible.   [I am not invisible.]

The conversation between Ana and Ernesto took the form of bilingual couplets that employed the poetry of these students' full linguistic repertoires while offering a complex critique about their own ideas of citizenship. As they passed the writing between them, they began to help each other by finding rhymes in English and Spanish, at times turning to Google Translate on Ernesto's phone to check Spanish spelling and orthography. As they spoke about the writing, they communicated bilingually, sharing images and stories, and also finding that they identified with each others' languages and experiences.

Translanguaging Writing

The suggestions below are adapted from Maisha T. Fisher's valuable *Writing in Rhythm: Spoken Word Poetry in Urban Classrooms*. The steps have been adjusted to address bilingualism for those teaching bilingual students or introducing translanguaging writing workshop activities that involve sharing writing, interaction, direct feedback, and building confidence.

- Hold "read and feed" in-class writing workshops that produce both content and feedback immediately through silent reading of a shared text, followed by direct comments. The author being reviewed must listen to the feedback and take notes. At the end of the feedback period, the author may ask questions and clarify her work.

- Address the politics of bilingualism and "Standard American English" globally and historically. Documentaries and texts about students learning English are important for opening up discussions about subtractive English Only policies that harm bilingual learning.

- Introduce and build bilingual vocabulary. Practicing words and phrases from different languages in classrooms can highlight the expertise of bilingual students and give emergent bilingual students confidence that their home languages are valued by their teachers and classmates.

- Encourage students to translanguage, to express their truths through original prose and verse using more than one language. The bilingual experiences of students learning English can inspire writing that is both expressive and critical. Invite students to see the poetic potential of their bilingual voices—to understand the musicality, beauty, and cadences of different languages.

- Offer opportunities for revision and reinforcement.

- Be respectful of students when engaging in discussions and providing encouragement.

- Approach bilingualism openly.

- Confer with groups of students to coach them on assignments and projects.

- Consult with individual students for past and future steps in assignments and projects.

Ana and Ernesto directly link identity and translanguaging in a powerful poem that not only questions misconceptions, stereotypes, and ideas of citizenship and labor, but also musically syncs rhythms into a single song. This is the beauty of creative activities that encourage students to write together; they are flexible and allow for immediate sharing of writing and authorship.

The most important aspect of write-around activities, however, is the power to spark dialogues, stories, and identifications among writers and readers. The collecting and sharing of stories quickly becomes a literacy project that has the potential to tap into the local community and engage students with their lived experiences as they become critically aware of their lives as topics for research. In other words, when students begin to view their own lives from the perspective of a researcher, their everyday realities seem strange and new. This reorientation causes them to narrate their own and others' stories in a new way, as students learn to use their voice and authority, and gain confidence in representing their communities and expertise from their lives. Such projects engage parents and local communities in conversations about educational goals, motivations, and the ways reading and writing are used expressively in community literacy projects.

Community Writing Bridges: Student Writers Bringing Communities into Classrooms

M'ijo, mis sueños ya mero se completan,   [My son, my dreams are about to come true]
my first son has created his own life,
living a life I never had,
I have given you a roof, food, and clothes,
now it is your choice,
to see a world I never saw.

M'ijo, my home is far away,   [My son]
ya mero se termina mi vida aquí   [my time in this place is almost done]
we are leaving you,
just as a mother bird leaves her children,
our lives are back in our home
this is your home now, not ours.

From my parents' words I know
there is an unknown world that awaits me,
without guidance, it is my choice,
without a goal, it is my failure,
without a voice, I am alone.

    This is the advice I gave myself.

Eighteen-year-old KUL member Marco wrote this poem shortly before he graduated high school. In the first two stanzas, Marco channels the voices of his parents, which connect to his own voice that emerges in the last stanza, as a son becoming a man, living a life built on the sacrifices of his parents to move ahead and attend college. The poem initially took shape from a writing exercise that asked each student to bring family photos to write about in order to practice description. Flipping through his cell phone, Marco found photos of each of his parents taken individually, and from these he built his first two stanzas. The poem balances between voices, but also features a rhythmic quality as the voices mingle with one another into the half-lines' repetition in the last stanza. Marco's parents planned on returning to Mexico shortly after he graduated, which contributed much of the emotional weight he experienced writing this poem.

Initially, Marco was hesitant to share this poem with members of KUL because he thought it was too personal. He eventually did share it, though, and it became a favorite poem for readers of the student anthology. After sharing it, he realized he was not alone in this experience, as all the KUL students had deep familial connections that stretched across nations, sometimes living divided from one or both parents.

The photograph writing exercise draws from research into cultural memory and the role photography can play in articulating it. Annette Kuhn argues that photography is useful to connect social and individual memory of stories. According to Kuhn, "Personal and family photographs figure importantly in cultural memory, and memory work with photographs offers a particularly productive route to understanding the social and cultural aspects of memory" (283). Writing can pave the way for connecting social and individual memories, and family artifacts like photos can become sites for family research and literacy learning.

Photographs can speak for the present and past, but they also have the power to give voice to the future, as we can see in Marco's example. Rather than look to the past for stories in the photographs, Marco turned to the present and future, seeing his story as a part of his parents' story, as an additional chapter in the family history. One also senses in the poem the struggles of emergent bilingualism, as the voices of the poem gradually speak more English, arriving at the poet's voice by the final lines.

Another KUL student felt inspired by an image to create a work of nonfiction prose. A twelfth grader at the time, and now a student at a local community college, Eliana found inspiration in several images of

Photos of Eliana's mother that inspired her to write "A Day I Will Never Forget."

her mother working as a food vendor during a county fair (see the photo on the previous page). Eliana's piece, entitled "A Day I Will Never Forget," moved from the photographs of her mother to a specific narrative involving an accident she witnessed, one that forever shaped her appreciation for her mother's central role in her family. This is the text in full:

A Day I Will Never Forget

I started to look for my mom as soon as I heard the explosion. I could feel fear creeping up every part of me. I caught a glimpse of my mom, a tear came streaming down my face. It seemed as if in the blink of an eye, everyone ran towards her. I stood there in shock, feeling like a complete *idiota* for not being able to help her out. *Do something!* As my mouth filled with a bitter taste, I ran toward my mom. By the time I got to her my face was soaked in tears.

"*¡Mamá!*"

"*¡Ayudarla!* Help her!" someone screamed.

"Get some water! *¡Agua! Agua!*"

"Help! Help! *¡Ayuda!*"

"*¡Mamá, mamá!*"

I cried out to her, and she told me not to be scared. But how could I? Only fear, that's all I felt, for the one who I loved most in this world.

Flashback to a few months earlier, July 2008. The fair was coming up and my mom was investigating what she needed to become a food vendor. She knew this could be a big way to expand the Mexican restaurant she had built by herself. All I knew was that she was going to need a couple thousand dollars to pull off the whole thing. Since she had met all of the legal and health requirements she needed, it was time for my family to get prepared for some hard work up ahead. We were first-timers to all this commotion selling food at the fair. After spending a whole afternoon and night setting up our booth, we were ready to start selling authentic *comida Mexicana* [Mexican food].

One of my mom's friends offered us his gas broiler so we could roast *al pastor* visible to the public. My mom didn't think twice in accepting the offer, but none of us knew what we needed to be very careful setting up this sort of appliance. Since it was a last minute addition, we hooked it up as best as we knew. On the fourth day of the fair, we were still having a lot of trouble with troubleshooting all the business we generated. Our food was a hit, but we were completely new and still learning the ropes. Other vendors had the advantage of years of experience. My mom was turning the *al pastor* when suddenly a loud explosion caught her on fire. Before I could even analyze what had just happened, someone else had already come to the rescue and put her out.

Sometimes I would just lie on my bed and cry and reproach myself for not running to help her when it happened. I would pray to God and ask him why *¿Mamá? ¿Mamá?* It killed me inside to even think about the pain she was going through. I wish it would have been me instead of her. All along I had never realized how important my mother was to me until this happened.

Why do tragic things have to happen for people to understand the importance of others? After the accident, my aunt took care of my mom. My brother, sister, and I went to work at the restaurant. We couldn't afford to have it closed down, especially with all the expenses we had to cover for my mother's care. While we worked I knew it crossed everyone's minds how my mother took on so much every day at work. It took three of us to do all the work she did on her own. I was amazed. I admired my mom's strength. She had the courage to get up every day and go to work for our well-being even if it meant she had to be in pain. That's something worthy to look up to.

A short while after this tragic experience, I knew that I didn't want to disappoint my mother, and I wanted to become someone with a bright future. It is for her that I want to accomplish great things in life and further my education. I want to be someone that inspires many people, just like she inspired me.

Eliana's text had complex narrative features, including shifting points of view, multiple voices, and a creatively organized timeline with a flashback sequence. Like Marco, Eliana focused on her family, and she practiced storytelling as she composed the text, later sharing this story in the published KUL anthology. Eliana used Spanish in this text sparingly, saving it for when characters called for *ayuda* and *agua*, for describing the style of marinated pork called *al pastor*, and for referring to her mother, *Mamá*. Combined with the images, the story became Eliana's tribute to her mother, and also a compelling portrait of a family coming to grips with a disaster and moving forward together. Eliana's photovoice composition took the shape of a story, one that also became an expressive family artifact. Like Marco's, Eliana's family photographs triggered a stream of writing. In the several pieces she included in the KUL anthology, she experimented with genres, points of view, and bilingualism. Later, Eliana told me that she translated the story to the best of her ability in Spanish for her mother so she could email it to her family in Mexico.

For younger students, photography can produce similarly expressive, social narratives by showing communities in local spaces like workplaces, schools, and the domestic spaces of families. Ten-year-old Lisa composed the following text at VBL by researching Google images related to a memory she had in mind about her family. In this case, Lisa imagined the photograph that she would search for, and included what she found. Below the photo, she gave her reasoning for selecting the image. The text reads:

Horses are fun to ride. I rode a horse last year. My dad used to work at Churchill Downs. I rode Stephanie and Susie when I was eight. I rode Dandy last year. I fed them grapes and they liked it. My whole family likes horses too. I like donkeys too. Susie was black. Stephanie and Dandy were brown. I would like to have my own horse someday.

Lisa's photo text about horses.

Horses are fun to ride. I rode a horse last year. My dad used to work at Churchill Downs. I rode Stephanie and Susie when I was eight. I rode Dandy last year. I fed them grapes and they liked it. My whole family likes horses too. I like donkeys too. Susie was black. Stephanie and Dandy are brown. I would like to have my own horse someday.

Lisa connected her father's work history to her passion for horses, including the names of specific horses and describing her experiences at one of the most famous racetracks in the world. Lisa's memory triggered images in her mind of the horse she found to accompany her text. Another layer to this project would be for Lisa to research family photographs to learn more history about her family's connections to the horsing industry in Kentucky, directly examining further community links to horses, and especially uses of Spanish in these spaces. Already, we can imagine the funds of knowledge Lisa's community could offer Kentucky classrooms regarding one of the state's most important industries.

These types of images, when combined with interviews with family members, can become narrative starters for building stories that speak to family strengths—in Lisa's case, experience working in the horsing industry, as well as firsthand experience with many horses, jockeys, and owners. An archive of family photographs could become a rich resource for practicing description through writing while conducting additional field research. Photography assignments connected to writing should also encourage students to take additional photographs. In Lisa's case, this would mean encouraging her to take new photographs of horses or even assigning timeline exercises that would build on a series of photos in sequence. Because Lisa composed this work in English, I would also invite Spanish into the project—for example, by including transcripts of Spanish-language interviews about photographs.

As in the photovoice examples of Marco, Eliana, and Lisa, emergent bilingual students bring a wealth of community experiences and resilience that can cultivate positive attitudes toward schooling, uncovered by research that makes person-to-person contact the focus of writing. Language arts teachers of all levels stand to gain *confianza* by engaging students' communities in classrooms and organizing writing projects, like these, that fit the practices of emergent bilingual communities. In the next section of this chapter, I focus on the voice of Eduardo, who confidently challenges his readers to see the difficul-

Classroom and Community Practices

- Connect educators and community outreach programs in early stages of US schooling.

- Be open to different languages and make room for creative uses of all languages.

- Build trust with students' communities and ties to the different origins of families.

- Emphasize the power of all communities to recognize and confront language discrimination.

- Promote the path to college. No age is too young!

- Compliment the work of families and communities.

- . Make time and have patience.

ties he faces, while also testifying to the resilience of his community in the face of political debates about immigration. As Eduardo shares, immigration status need not be an additional obstacle blocking the educational opportunities of emergent bilingual students.

"Don't Throw Me Obstacles Throw Me Opportunities and You'll See What I Can Do": Listening to Emergent Bilingual Voices

I turn here to a translingual poem that touches on the lived experiences of emergent bilingual students who are immigrants. Eighteen-year-old Eduardo, a KUL poet born in Mexico but raised since age three in Kentucky, composed the poem. Eduardo was a member of KUL for two years and contributed creative work to the group's self-published anthology—in fact, he was the first of all KUL students to submit a polished text he had workshopped for weeks.

Eduardo's powerful text was a favorite of KUL students, and this made him proud—not only because he'd spent considerable time and effort on it, but more important, because the poem spoke to the topic of comprehensive reform for the millions of undocumented immigrants living and working in the United States.

don't cross the line

Sí, nosotros cruzamos la frontera,   [Yes, we crossed the border,]
pero that doesn't give you the right   [but]
    to cross the line and judge us.
We are an example of people
    fighting for happiness.
We can do anything we want
    as long as we put our mind to it.
    ¡Sí se puede¡   [Yes we can!]
    ¡Sí se puede¡   [Yes we can!]
You call us lazy
say we come here to do nothing
    but have anchor babies
but without us you wouldn't have America,
    you wouldn't have our labor.
This nation was built on immigrant blood
Mi familia y yo hemos hecho de este país   [My family and I have made this country]
tu piensas that only   [you think]
    because I come from somewhere
    else
I have no right to succeed in life.
Give me a notebook and a pencil,
    I'll write you my story.

When you read it, you'll realize
    that my life isn't easy
    and if you live it
you'd be grateful not to have lived
    what I've lived.

Si quieren que seamos mejor en este país,   [If you want us to be better here,]
    denos la oportunidad   [give us the opportunity]
    de demonstrarles   [to demonstrate]
    de lo que somos   [we are]
    capaces.   [capable.]

Give me the opportunity to show you
    that I can be
    as great as you, as your
    parents, and as your president
I am capable of doing everything
    you can do,
    but it's harder for me.
Why? Because of obstacles history threw at me.
Don't throw me obstacles throw me opportunities
and you'll see what I can do.

    Solo quiero triunfar,   [I only want to succeed,]
    y ahora me quieren deportar   [and now they want to deport me]
    y yo no quiero trabajar,   [and I don't want to work,]
    yo voy a luchar, yo voy a triunfar.   [I will fight, I will succeed.]
      ¡Ya nomás!   [Enough!]

Eduardo told me this was not the first poem he had published, but the first one he had written bilingually. Eduardo's first published poem had appeared in the high school literary magazine: "The other one was a love poem. I'm not sure how this [poem] would have gone over for that [magazine]," he said. "I think that and what I wrote would have probably caused some problems for a few people if I read it there. And Spanish too. Only if there was a little bit of Spanish is okay, but I used a lot of Spanish." I asked Eduardo why he felt comfortable sharing it with the KUL members. "Well," he said, "a lot of us live this situation or know people who do. It helps us to know we're not alone. So we don't give up. It makes us feel good to hear our language and situation."

Eduardo was committed to the KUL book project. Not only was he the first student to submit a polished poem, but he also served as a first reader for several of his friends who also submitted their writing. Eduardo's leadership in the project extended to organizing public readings and distributing copies of the book to elementary, middle, and high schools around the city.

Eduardo completed three workshop sessions with his poem over the course of four weeks and consulted me individually via email and Facebook messages during the same timeframe. The workshops where KUL students discussed his work sparked important discussions that touched upon the family lives of several KUL members or their friends. The real interests of students and the issues they dared not speak about during their classes became critical to building communities who shared struggles and acknowledged the precarious situation of millions of undocumented immigrants living in and contributing to the United States.

According to Eduardo, his initial drafts of the poem were written as prose during one of the workshops. Students began each workshop with timed freewriting exercises, which they later reviewed for notes for writing texts in different genres, including poetry, as was the case for Eduardo. The particular exercise that resulted in Eduardo's poem was a timed freewrite responding to the topic of immigration. After every minute, students were instructed to "switch languages" and write in another tongue for a minute before switching again. "I had never tried anything like that before," Eduardo remembered. "It was cool, I could follow my thoughts even when I changed languages."

In another workshop, students scoured their notes and freewrites for kernels of text to polish. Once Eduardo discovered the theme of immigration in his notes, he isolated some lines that he enjoyed and began to craft his poem. Eduardo chose a first-to-second-person address as a way of speaking directly to an audience who rarely saw the world from his perspective, of engaging in a call to dialogue with his readers. In that version of the poem, Eduardo varied his use of line enjambment and Spanish. The Spanish in Eduardo's poem showed pride in a community organized from the shadows and a history of shared struggle among Latin American immigrants to the United States.

In "don't cross the line," Eduardo writes about his desire to express himself and share his story—establishing a bilingual voice that calls out, seeking responses across languages: "Give me a notebook and a pencil, / I'll write you my story. / When you read it you'll realize / that my life isn't easy." The sharing of struggles as writing was important to him, and as someone who has listened to Eduardo, I can say that the sharing of these experiences, of collective struggle, is the first step toward healing and devising a plan of action—with *confianza* from the right mentors, of course. Sharing stories of struggles, as well as reading about similar stories, was the inspiration for Eduardo's poetic exploration and his bilingual call to action. Eduardo's call is one educators must respond to, and I ask, where do we begin? How can we learn more to help talented students like Eduardo?[3]

Certainly, we can recognize the complex and dynamic nature of bilingualism in Eduardo's poetic voice. We also see a critical recognition of his community's labor as fundamental to the wealth of the United States. The contribution of immigrant labor in Kentucky and so many other parts of the United States is a potential subject for further exploration and connection to academic content related to local literacy practices. The intersections of food production, literacy, photography, social justice, and emergent bilingualism are rich material for writing projects at all grade levels.

Writing projects that involve local perspectives and funds of knowledge, as well as student research, can lead to longer-term, more complex projects. In addition, multimodal projects that require students to combine words and images, in both their presentation of research sources and their own composition, invite them to explore dynamic ways of synthesizing and communicating information. For educators with the luxury of time, a portfolio project of student work—perhaps in the form of self-published books, a series, or as in the case of KUL students, an anthology—could become a text to share with other students and members of the community. Projects that relate directly to students' communities, especially research projects, could also present opportunities for dialogues with students' work.

Eduardo offers a test for all educators with these lines at the end of his poem: "Don't throw me obstacles throw me opportunities / and you'll see what I can do." He challenges his audience to provide equity, powerfully critiquing a tradition of exclusion. Just before these lines, he writes, "I am capable of doing everything you can do, / but it's harder for me. / Why? Because of obstacles history threw at me." Eduardo acknowledges his social constraints, but also expresses his own potential and confidence in his ability to meet challenges imposed upon him. His bilingualism and his participation in the KUL community guide him to meet obstacles head-on. Eduardo acknowledges power differences, and he asks his audience to do the same. He seems to imagine an audience unaware of its privilege amid suffering.

Eduardo's narrative in the poem is representative of emergent bilingual students in Kentucky, but it is also meaningful for all students in the United States who are learning about citizenship, opportunity, and inequality. Eduardo was indeed a capable young man, someone who acknowledged the strength of his community with a social consciousness. In our local communities, students like Eduardo call for our involvement and mentorship as educators, and as educators, we must respond with *confianza*.

I emphasize the resilience of language-minoritized communities, and I encourage more conversations that begin with poems like Eduardo's. Teachers seeking to extend their classrooms into communities must first examine the translanguaging tactics used by students in these communities to complete monolingual writing assignments. To craft literacy assignments that fit the practices of communities, educators must meet these communities halfway, first learning how students are already using their linguistic repertoires before finding ways to increase communication. As you will learn, language-minoritized communities who organize around education are incredibly resilient in the face of obstacles thrown by history, as Eduardo puts it.

The next chapter builds further on the notion of resilience in emergent bilingual communities amid standardized assessments that hinder their students. In the midst of so-called "official English" debates waged against families and communities, bilingualism becomes pivotal for sustaining history, culture, and identity. English Only, as we will see, is not the only perspective, unless it succeeds in narrowing perspectives so as to exclude the gifts of a democratic multilingual nation. Community-school collaborative literacy projects that explore and assess how students move their languages across different contexts will be attuned to students' linguistic repertoires, while also engaging them in critical analysis of the power dynamics of English Only arguments.

Chapter Five

Bilingual Community Funds of Knowledge and Formative Assessment: Beyond English Only

When I started to realize there was a language barrier
I was in kindergarten. I couldn't understand the songs
everyone felt so joyful singing. When they started taking
me out of class to get help learning English,
I felt so relieved that someone understood my struggle.
I felt so happy when I could ask my classmates to play
with me, and they no longer saw me as an outsider.
With two languages, I have two perspectives inside me that guide me.
Con dos idiomas dentro de mi hay dos perspectivas que me guían.

—Melina, *"Mi Perspectiva"*

"*Mi Perspectiva*," written by sixteen-year-old KUL member Melina, reflects the importance of self-assessment for language-minoritized students who not only experience institutional benchmarks for learning English, but also form their own standards for language learning from their bilingual lived experiences. Melina remembered her English immersion in kindergarten as both frightening and confusing, as she became conscious of a "language barrier" that made her feel like "an outsider" because she could not participate in sing-alongs or ask to play with her classmates. Around the same time, Melina found comfort in Spanish support, which eased her anxieties and increased her confidence. Melina writes that she gained confidence as others began to understand her efforts to become bilingual: "someone understood my struggle." With the relief offered by Spanish support, she felt emboldened to express herself openly and bilingually. In her poem, we can clearly see her translanguaging in the last two lines, providing English and Spanish versions of the same sentiment: "With two languages, I have two perspectives inside me that guide me. / *Con dos idiomas dentro de mi hay dos perspectivas que me guían.*" This ingenious couplet defines the thesis of the bilingual "*Mi Perspectiva*," representing in two languages what struggling and learning bilingually have taught Melina about her own strengths as a student and a person who is negotiating her view of the world.

"*Mi Perspectiva*" displays an important aspect of self-assessment and—importantly—Melina's use of both languages to demonstrate that assessment. Melina's bilingual verbal rhythms find vivid expression in the final couplet, but as she writes in the English section of her poem, becoming bilingual through English immersion shook her confidence, causing her to question her ability to feel like she belonged at school or to find a space to be bilingual. As a high school student over a decade later, Melina had certainly overcome much of what she recognized as initial educational hardships, and her confidence as a student was grounded in the community she built with KUL. The community had given Melina and her fellow KUL members a break from high-stakes testing and the kind of competitive nature that characterizes schools these days, where students judge themselves in comparison to their peers. This race to be number one was something that KUL students questioned, and that contributed to their shaky confidence with literacy.

The competitive regimes of schools encourage

I Win, an illustration by homework tutor Monica.

students to strive to be at the top of the class—a very real issue for bilingual students, as shown in the drawing (on the previous page) *I Win* by eighteen-year-old Monica, where students climb over one another, fighting tooth and nail to get to the candy gumballs. I tutored alongside Monica at an after-school program in New York City, where we both saw how the logic of meritocracy standardized individualism at the expense of community. For Monica, the image illustrated how the race to the top starts early for children, with limited spoils for those willing to step on others to achieve their ends. When assessment manifests as intense competition, students learning English are left unable to compete on a level playing field with their classmates whose home language matches that of their schools. Whether you're in Kentucky or New York, getting stepped on hurts, but what hurts me most as an educator is when students accept the idea that this failure is a result of their own shortcomings.

What fascinates me as a language educator interested in community literacies is what Melina's narrative teaches us about assessment. Through this piece, Melina assesses her own experience as a learner, drawing us into her understanding and telling a story about her journey—information we clearly would not learn through a standardized assessment that measured only English proficiency. Specifically, in the last two lines of her poem, Melina articulates the importance of guides and their impact on her learning. In Melina's case, these guides take the form of her dual languages ("With two languages, I have two perspectives inside me that guide me. / *Con dos idiomas dentro de mi hay dos perspectivas que me guían.*"). I wonder what this concept might teach us about assessment for multilingual students: How do we understand Melina's bilingual perspective when teaching writing? More generally, how can we assess the linguistic repertoires of our students if we focus solely on English? What is our role as teachers in understanding how communities guide our pedagogies? How do we escape the traps of language standardization that confine bilingual students' gifts and stories?

In this chapter, I illustrate how students experience this silencing, through director David Levien's 2009 short film *Immersion*. *Immersion* does an effective job of illustrating Angela Valenzuela's notion of "subtractive schooling" by portraying how emergent bilingual students cope with English Only assessments that subtract home languages. The film poignantly depicts an elementary school student's struggle against standardized tests offered only in English because of state reforms imposing structured English immersion policies. Rather than create national unity, English Only sustains the educational inequalities that punish bilingualism without truly taking into account the day-to-day struggles experienced by affected students. *Immersion* humanizes the discourse surrounding the smokescreen of official English branded as "English for the Children," showing what bilingual education for children really looks like. I go into further detail about *Immersion* in this chapter and offer examples of students who were inspired to respond to language assessment in ways similar to those portrayed in the film.

This film and these examples connect my argument about the importance of *confianza* to issues of assessment. Educators and community groups can learn from one another, building the kinds of relationships that are of utmost importance for the future of our students and honoring all communities' languages. To build these relationships, we must make assessment transparent and accessible to diverse communities and create dialogues about assessment that move beyond English Only policies that discount the diversity of American voices. As I argue, the aspects of community included in NCTE assessment frameworks should be updated to reflect the funds of knowledge of bilingual families and formative assessment models. I suggest that teachers need to know how to listen to emergent bilingual students and their stories about language development and bicultural identity when developing content and language objectives.

Official English and English Immersion

The *NCTE Position Paper on the Role of English Teachers in Educating English Language Learners* emphasizes that "teachers need to consider content objectives as well as English language development objectives" (p. xi). But as teachers, we also need to know the stories of our students' communities. Maybe you've never considered how emergent bilingual students' senses of bicultural identity and community shape your teaching. If this is so, then I hope you begin to define for yourself what it means to be sensitive to emergent bilingual students and connected to their personal contexts. And as you develop assessment strategies for these students, I hope you can begin to imagine their bilingualism as a different standard, one that can be improved on at all grade levels. I ask you to rethink assessment for emergent bilingual students like Melina. However, I understand that there are larger forces that impinge upon our classrooms and standardize our pedagogies for high-stakes testing. I now turn to one of these forces: official English.

In 1998, California voters passed Proposition 227, the "English for the Children" initiative, mandating that state school systems would teach literacy to "limited English proficient" students via English Only immersion programs not normally expected to exceed one year, rather than providing any funding for bilingual public education. Until its repeal in November 2016, this policy of structured English immersion permitted only one year of bilingual instruction for tens of thousands of emergent bilingual students assessed as "limited" in their academic English proficiency. When implemented, this policy removed students from bilingual classes and placed them in structured English immersion programs or transitional English classrooms on the way to mainstream language arts classes. With Proposition 227 and *limited* bilingual support from schools, students were on their own to sink or swim. At the time, roughly a quarter of California's students were classified as English language learners.

Bilingual education faces an uphill battle with this kind of English Only legislation, which views the home languages of students as "gaps" rather than opportunities. The word *limited* in the LEP designation carries the stigma of deficiency, not only in terms of students' bilingual abilities, but also in assumptions about students' potential and opportunities. But what would happen if, as I advocate in this book, instead of marking students by their limitations, teachers could instead judge them by their translingual potential, and especially by the gifts from their communities that they carry into classrooms?

Rather than assume that emerging bilingual students are limited in their abilities or lacking in their efforts, we must recognize that they are not limited within their own community contexts, but their bilingualism is minoritized by institutional beliefs that favor monolingualism. If we shift to a translingual pedagogy, we stop blaming "gaps" in English Only literacy on students or their parents. Instead, we look to the diverse linguistic repertoires of students who are building communities despite the prevalence of ideologies that dismiss those communities. As one would expect, within this harsh political climate, community programs across the United States are beginning to organize and mobilize to promote their shared interests—especially the need for equitable education that recognizes that English Only expectations are not realistic in a global economy. As I've suggested throughout this book, community resources are often more effective in supporting emergent bilingualism because they are not held to the same standards as formal, accredited schools, and because they focus on the assets students bring to the table. Given the efficacy of such community services in developing and maintaining bilingualism, their scarcity reflects a pressing need.

Unfortunately, California Proposition 227 is not alone. Thirty-one states have similar official English policies on record. NCTE has explicitly critiqued deficit-oriented language in English education, and its research policy brief *English Language Learners* acknowledges that such statewide English Only initiatives are not backed by research or even intuition with regard to bilingualism. From the monolingualist perspective of official English, bilingualism hinders unity and sows the seeds for a polyglot nation, something that is seen as negative. Among certain sectors of the American population, therefore, bilingualism is valued less than "native" English fluency and literacy. Ironically, many of these same official English advocates do believe bilingualism can be beneficial (perhaps even for their own children)—as long as English is the home language—and encourage their students to learn a second language, such as French or Mandarin, at earlier and earlier ages. Nevertheless, this view of bilingualism as additive for a privileged few still fails to recognize emergent bilingual students' full linguistic repertoires and practices.

Building on Moments of Resilience: Translanguaging in *Immersion*

The film *Immersion* relates the real-life dilemmas faced by emergent bilingual students during subtractive English Only examinations. These examinations deceptively measure monolingualism only, in effect dismissing bilingual aptitudes. *Immersion* captures well the traumatizing effects of language alienation on vulnerable students during testing, something that has been well researched by scholars:

> When a bilingual individual confronts a monolingual test, developed by monolingual individuals, and standardized and normed on a monolingual population, both the test-taker and the test are asked to do something that they can't. The bilingual test-taker can't perform like a monolingual. The monolingual test can't "measure" in the other language.
>
> Ironically, single-language tests deceptively measure the "monolingual" part of the bilingual (one or the other of the bilingual's two languages), irrespective of proficiency in that language, and they do so reliably. But these tests fail insofar as they may exclude mental content that is available to the bilingual in the other language, and mental processes and abilities that are the product of bilingualism. (Valdés, *Expanding Definitions of Giftedness* 176)

I have emphasized the importance of acknowledging the hybrid nature of the everyday practices of emergent bilingual individuals and communities, even amid policies that seek to subtract home languages and stigmatize difference. In such cases, translanguaging becomes a form of resilience and social justice. *Immersion* dramatizes the day-to-day practices of an emergent bilingual student and how he deals with cultural assumptions that value monolingualism. The film offers a window into this experience from a student's point of view and can be an important conversation starter for our work with emergent bilingual students.

Immersion narrates the perspectives of students and educators learning to communicate bilingually in an English Only context. (If you have 13 minutes, take the time to watch it—even before you read this section. You can find it at www.immersionfilm.com.) Set in California after the passage of Proposition 227, the film shows ten-year-old Moisés failing in standardized testing as he becomes submerged in an English Only climate that subtracts the language of his family and his own voice. The official website for the film reads, "Using untrained child actors from public schools in the San Francisco Bay Area, 'Immersion' plunges its audience into the visceral experience of a child who cannot understand his teacher. The film puts a human face on the debate about the education of English Language Learners." *Immersion* offers a window into how students' literacy practices align and conflict with the literacies promoted by legislation and institutionalized in schools.

A significant amount of the film's dialogue is in Spanish with English sub-titles, and it depicts several instances of mistranslation, language brokering, and translingual dexterity. During a telling scene in the film, Moisés, who sits near the back of the classroom, solves the mathematical equation for an orally delivered word problem, and opens a bilingual dictionary to look up the English transla-tion for the resulting number before his English-dominant classmates can solve the task—save for one student, a bully named Enrique who has copied the answer over Moisés's shoulder. Enrique raises his hand and gives the stolen answer while Moisés searches for the translation in his dictionary. Enrique is unable, however, to offer an explanation to the teacher, Ms. Peterson, about how he arrived at his answer.

Sensing his moment, Moisés apprehensively raises his hand. Ms. Peterson rushes to him.

"Yes, Moisés."

He surveys all the eyes of his classmates turning toward him from right to left. This appears to be the first time he has raised his hand in class.

"Forty," he says in a quiet, high-pitched voice.

Ms. Peterson moves closer to Moisés. "Yes, that's right, very good." She ex-amines the scratch paper on his desk. Ms. Peterson meets his eyes. "Great, can you tell us how you got that?"

"Forty," Moisés says, his voice slightly cracking. A few laughs can be heard in the background.

"Yep, very good. Can you explain to the class what you did here? How you got that?"

There is a long pause, and Moisés sees all eyes on him. "Forty," he says, nearly whispering. The other students laugh again, this time much louder and in unison.

Ms. Peterson hands Moisés back his paper, and as she walks back to the front of the class, she overhears another student named Joe saying, "That kid's so dumb."

"Joe, do you want to lose your recess?" Ms. Peterson threatens.

The laughter dies down.

Moisés hangs his head.

As he continues to fail the word problem portions of his practice exams, Moisés also experiences playground bullying from his classmates. When playing kickball, he does not hear an English rule about "no tagging" after kicks, so, when called out, he disputes the call in Spanish. Moisés realizes that no one understands him, or that they all pretend not to understand him—whichever, it does not mat-ter. He runs away from the game to sit alone with his math book.

Moisés's older brother Luis is a custodian at the school, and he stops to cheer his brother on about his math exam for a moment. The aforementioned bully, Enrique, uses this moment to pester Moisés again, purposefully tossing trash on the ground in front of Luis and saying, "Luis, there's some trash there." Moisés rises in fury, but Luis calms the situation, picking up the balled paper, disposing of it, and sitting down with Moisés again. Luis assures his brother that Enrique is half the student Moisés is, and that, when it comes to mathematics, this bully can't compete. Luis has seen how hard Moisés studies, but he has not seen Moisés struggle during class.

Moisés meets his classmate Gerardo shortly after this exchange. In Spanish, Gerardo points out why students who do not speak English should not take the standardized exams. It seems he has overheard the principal say in a telephone conversation that this would be better for the school's overall testing scores. Instead, Gerardo suggests to Moisés that the two should go to the park and have ice cream.

At this pivotal point in *Immersion*, Moisés has a choice to make. Does he take a test he knows he will fail, or does he go for ice cream in the park with his friend Gerardo? As Moisés considers his options, he experiences a flashback: It's nighttime, windy, and Moisés has jumped over a fence, as his mother calls out to him that she's caught on a wire. He helps her down and the two tumble to the ground. When his frightened mother asks if he's okay, Moisés jokes that their experience is like a game, and she pats him on the shoulder before telling him to run. The flashback quickly ends as Moisés continues to look at himself in the mirror. He tells Gerardo that he is sorry, but he must take the test. Gerardo shakes his head and goes to the park on his own.

The flashback episode reveals a great deal about Moisés: how his mother and he migrated to the United States, that he bases important choices on his family, and how—despite failure and an imposing political climate throwing obstacles at him—he maintains the hope that he will succeed. Putting a human face on the obstacles that students like Moisés encounter is important to counter subtractive, deficit-oriented approaches to learning English, and also to understand that all students carry their communities in their identities, as well as the resilience that marks the dignity of these communities.

For Moisés, his community is his immediate family and a few Spanish-speaking students in his class. Each time I watch this film, I wonder how Moisés would be affected by a program like VBL, how a larger community of students and mentors to speak with would build his confidence, how he could feel *confianza* with bilingual students and caring adults who shared his experiences. This film gives educators a glimpse of what subtractive "English for the Children" schooling looks like in practice as it silences intelligent emergent bilingual students.

Each time I've shown this film to students at KUL and VBL, they have found the plight of Moisés personally relatable. Lee, a fourteen-year-old African American student I tutored at VBL, said, "I seen that bullying ESL kids before. And you look at him [Moisés], and he's the smartest kid in class, and they treat him so mean because he the new kid and don't speak English." In this respect of being "the new kid," Lee said she could relate, as she had shared similar experiences when moving to Kentucky from Tennessee several years prior.

I have also shown the film in my university classes, where the majority of students identified themselves as monolingual English speakers. In large part, they were not familiar with the struggles of emergent bilingual students like Moisés. In a written response to the film, one university student from the Appalachian region of Kentucky wrote:

> I never really thought about the kids who speak Spanish taking tests and not being able to understand what was being asked. I felt really bad watching Moisés struggle taking the test and I didn't realize why they couldn't give him a test in Spanish, or just have someone translate for him. I felt really bad for Moisés and thought he should have been given a little help. I respect how Moisés decided not to skip the test even though he knew he was going to fail. I think he decided not to after having the flashbacks of him and his mom crossing the border, and realized how hard they worked to get there and he didn't want to mess up or jeopardize how much they put at risk trying to get where they are now. How to educate new immigrant children in the US is a huge topic right now and I believe that throwing them into the pot with all the other kids speaking just English is not an effective way. I believe that they should get a little more time and should not base how good they are at math on their first test taken in a new language. I really liked this movie.

Like this student, several of the other university students I showed *Immersion* to asked why Moisés would be in a class where only English was spoken; they felt that the policies set him up to fail and did not make any sense. The strong reactions and possibilities for change raised by this short film offer substantial content for writing activities, including opportunities for students to write from their own experiences and observations of classmates and institutions. Students who identify as monolingual English speakers learn to empathize with language-minoritized students finding resilience in their communities, and discuss their own ideas of what it means to be a bilingual American. Such conversations also encourage more inclusive appreciation for emergent bilingual families' translanguaging literacies, moving from an *English language learning* orientation to one of *emergent bilingualism*.

If we set up classrooms in certain ways, these kinds of writing moments and dialogues about official English policies can happen in K–12 settings, as well. I conducted a write-around response to *Immersion* with seven VBL students after they finished their homework one evening. The students ranged in age from ten to sixteen, and two were emergent bilingual writers. *Immersion* ends with Moisés taking the real exam he has been preparing for, his first test in the United States. The film does not show how Moisés performs on the test, instead leaving viewers to fill in the details of what happens when the story ends, based on their own expectations. I realized that continuing the narrative through writing would be an excellent activity, as the students responded to the end of the film by asking, "What happens next? Did he pass? Then what happens to Moisés? In five years? In ten?" I asked them to begin their explorations by writing their own answers to those questions.

The VBL students began with one line and then shared their writing with the student next to them, going around in a circle. The last student in the rotation provided a title for the text before returning it to the owner of the shared writing. This is the text that fourteen-year-old David produced with his workshop partners:

Esperando for Power

Moisés thinks he may have failed but he is a really smart boy and even tho he may go thro this but he will pass this problem and get stronger. Moisés gets very nervis because the test. He looks up at the teacher and raises his hand to go to the bathroom. When he is in the bathroom he sees himself again and his mom and now his dad and brother too. Then he thinks like he did before "*Que hacemos?* Who can told me the answers?" But suddenly he listen he thinks "*¿sí o no?*" Moisés decides that the best way to fight back is to get a good score on the next test and to believe in himself. He will go to collage and take a class with *el profe* Alvarez.

We all enjoyed that last line. Obviously, I would be honored to have Moisés in any writing class I taught—in my class, he would write about his family, his languages, his identity, and his visions for his community. The exercise not only brought in the rest of Moisés's family from the film, but it also opened students up to writing bilingually in the voice of the character—which the two bilingual students in the group did. When David read this version aloud, we asked the last student in the rotation, fourteen-year-old Stella, why she added the title "*Esperando* for Power." "Because," she said, "someday he will see that he is strong because some people believe in him. The Spanish is because he is still thinking and waiting in Spanish and going to English."

To clarify, I asked who cared about Moisés in the film, who saw him beyond his test scores.

"His teacher and his parents and his brother," Stella said.

"What if Moisés had VBL?" I asked the group.

"Then he wouldn't feel alone because he could speak in Spanish and get homework help in Spanish and learn English," David said.

Stella and David pointed to the partnerships that happen among students, families, and teachers, and how community programs like VBL and KUL can make the difference between students who fail exams and students who feel like failures. Students who bring that kind of resilience to school communities are one step ahead. And schools and teachers that open up assignments to allow this kind of work, work that openly acknowledges students' communities and their struggles, can help bilingual students even more. However, there are currently not enough films like *Immersion* to encourage this kind of work, especially in representing settings like Kentucky, which have recently begun to experience significant Latino/a settlement.

Communities and Assessment

The importance of community cannot be stressed enough in assessment, and, fortunately, NCTE has been at the forefront in advocating for this connection. Still, the link between assessment and emergent bilingual communities should be emphasized further. Number 9 of the "Standards for the Assessment of Reading and Writing" (SARW) by NCTE and IRA recognizes the importance of community for assessment. "Assessment," according to the SARW, "must be based in the local school learning community, including active and essential participation of families and community members" (Standard 9). Teachers indeed are primary agents and enforcers of assessment, and classrooms are the locations of our most important assessments. However, according to the SARW:

> The most effective assessment unit is the local school learning community. First, the collective experiences and values of the community can offer a sounding board for innovation and multiple perspectives to provide depth of understanding and to counter individual and cultural biases. Second, the involvement of all parties in assessment encourages a cooperative, committed relationship among them rather than an adversarial one. Third, because language learning is not restricted to what occurs in school, assessment must go beyond the school curriculum. (Standard 9)

Thus, the SARW argue that assessment should begin locally in the communities where schools are situated. The collective experiences, values, and wisdom of local communities are not only a "sounding board for innovation and multiple perspectives," but also the basis of shared funds of knowledge grounded in social relationships. Committed relationships *en confianza* are key, and safe spaces that host shared interests become communal rather than subtractive and competitive. Of course, competition can still become a topic of discussion, but as the SARW point out, students' learning is not restricted to school assessment. If this is so, what else might we do to go beyond school curricula into communities in order to make assessment truly a collaborative venture? What can we learn from partnering with bilingual community programs like VBL and KUL to form networks of service providers, mentors, educators, and schools connected to students across the nation?

The importance of building *confianza* around issues of assessment—between educators and communities, but especially with the families of our emergent bilingual students—cannot be stressed enough. The SARW state that "families must be involved as active, essential participants in the assessment process," detailing how to connect communities and schools in spaces outside of schools. According to the standards:

> In many schools, families stand on the periphery of the school community, some feeling hopeless, helpless, and unwanted. However, the more families understand their children's progress in school, the more they can contribute to that progress. If teachers are to understand how best to assist children from cultures that are different from their own, families are particularly important resources. Families must become, and be helped to become, active participants in the assessment process. (Standard 11)

The SARW drive home the point that families must become actively involved in assessment. This, of course, means all families, including immigrant and emergent bilingual parents. Without explicitly mentioning language-minoritized families, the SARW refer to families who are "on the periphery of the school community," or are still attempting to learn about how schooling operates, such as immigrant parents like those of the KUL and VBL students. The SARW advocate transparency in assessment with the intention of providing clear channels for family and community participation.

My suggestion is that we consider how immigrant and emergent bilingual parents already are demonstrating academic support. Though the SARW do value families as "important resources" for educators to learn how to help students, the standards still do not give sufficient credit to the ways parents "on the periphery" are already working to teach their children English, while simultaneously challenging their marginalization. It is undoubtedly true that language-minoritized parents sometimes self-consciously perceive their English proficiency as deficient, but it is also true that these same parents have deep convictions about the importance of English and seek out programs like KUL and VBL.

Also, assessment needs to be flexible enough to account for the rich language experiences and gifts students bring into classrooms and communities. Katie Van Sluys offers a definition of assessment that relates to *confianza* in students' communities and recognizes that assessment is not "one-way"—or monolingual, for that matter:

> Assessment is a collaborative and malleable process that transpires over time. It's not a one-way street with experts, internal or external, passing down information that tells a student where he or she stands; rather, assessment encompasses specific feedback that enables improvement that can be shared amongst a community of writers. (93)

Van Sluys, like the SARW, advocates for transparency. Indeed, transparency has special significance for parents unfamiliar with methods of written feedback on student reports or grading rubrics, let alone projects that extend over multiple weeks and end in portfolios. Sharing educators' specific ways of giving feedback with parent groups or organizations would open discussions that could help students craft their writing and give parents insight into methods of assessing language and literacy. Schools must have a role in developing these dialogues—and they might do so successfully by partnering with the thousands of after-school bilingual programs across the nation.

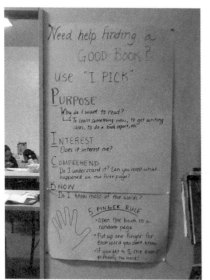

Poster project created by a Valle del Blue-grass Library volunteer for a university-level elementary education course, on display at the after-school program.

As a pedagogical opportunity, *confianza* can work to demystify school policies, procedures, and assessments—such as standardized tests and college readiness indicators—and increase school involvement, potentially improving communication between language-minoritized communities and schools at all grade levels. Community programs also benefit when educators share or help design teaching materials, offer workshops, make book recommendations, or even donate books. The photograph on this page, for example, shows a poster project for a university-level elementary education course displayed near the VBL bookcases. A future teacher repurposed the poster to assist VBL tutors and tutees in choosing appropriate books to read. The visual tool served as a quick measure for tutors, tutees, and other library patrons to evaluate books' suitability for reading practice.

In addition to starting conversations with families about assessment, teachers who support students in the kind of public writing suggested throughout this book are creating occasions for authentic assessment: by the real audiences who read the students' texts. As students create these texts, they build on community knowledge and exchange funds of knowledge with classmates. Projects like the KUL student anthology can also be important for students to proudly share their identity and expertise in the languages they feel comfortable with. Most important, however, is to consider extending the duration of assignments and using informal writing to understand, analyze, pose questions about, and affect the realities of students' lived experiences in their communities.

Designing these kinds of classroom projects as part of formative assessment means constructing lessons as a series, extending instruction across days and weeks.

Developing Assessment Strategies

The *NCTE Position Paper on the Role of English Teachers in Educating English Language Learners* offers a potential framework for developing assessment that addresses emergent bilingual students and how they build community. The position paper suggests a number of interactive ways teachers can demonstrate respect for the sociocultural learning of students becoming bilingual. Classroom strategies recommended by the position paper include classroom discussions, peer interactions, formative group projects, and regular practice in composing and sharing texts. These suggestions focus on student-centered literacy projects that are collaborative and promote students' confidence in their abilities to make valuable contributions with their literacy, such as group research on local communities that promotes discussion of differences and bilingualism. The position paper offers immediate actions language arts teachers can take in their classrooms:

- Assign cooperative, collaborative writing activities designed to promote discussion.

- Encourage all students to contribute and interact with peers to support each other's learning.

- Instead of drills and single-response exercises, give students time for writing practice (p. xiii).

I also suggest these actions:

- Provide students with sample portfolio assignments and assessment scores to demonstrate how the projects shape academic growth, to enhance motivation, and to help students maintain a timeline.

- Promote bilingualism and reassure families of its value for all learning.

- Distribute and discuss administrative bilingual assessments and evaluation measures, and encourage emergent bilingual students to share this information with their community programs.

Teachers can begin by adopting formative assessment practices in their lessons and locating funds of knowledge within students' research and group projects. Projects that involve authentic reading and writing experiences and offer textual strategies and models, as well as meaningful choices, are important for emergent bilingual students to build confidence and competencies—which are necessary for any meaningful assessment. Local literacies are valuable funds of knowledge that represent the dignity of every community.

Locating funds of knowledge means listening to students and what their research uncovers about their sense of belonging and communities. For educators who seek to explore how emergent bilingual students form communities through languages and literacies, assessing funds of knowledge means becoming aware of students' linguistic repertoires and building on them through specific, formative projects. Such projects should involve different forms of media and require emergent bilingual students to be decision makers in their composing process, and to discuss their bilingual choices and representations of communities in their texts.

Technology can be used as an aid for multimodal projects and collaborative learning environments that layer languages, either through subtitles or dubbed voice-over translations. Multimedia projects such as photo slideshows published on YouTube are excellent platforms for public multimodal compositions. Through tagging videos and sharing them on social networks, students can evaluate their audience reach based on the numbers of "likes" and views of a project. After publishing their work in the KUL anthology, students hashtagged posts and shared links to their writing and artwork via Facebook, Twitter, and Instagram. KUL students not only shared their work, but also engaged their expanding audience in comment exchanges and instant feedback.

Confidence in Funds of Knowledge for Assessment

Programs like KUL and VBL are spaces for communities to converse freely and form partnerships based on earned trust over time, across and beyond language differences. Nowhere is *confianza* more important than in assessment of emergent bilingual students, because these students need to trust that their bilingual voices are heard and celebrated—especially in an assessment world that seems overly competitive. Projects that make use of students' linguistic repertoires go beyond orthographic exercises that standardize rote skills.

The film *Immersion* teaches us that emergent bilingual students develop resilient practices beyond English Only standards. *Immersion* makes space for discussions about bilingual learning, official English policies, and community strengths. Though such policies attempt to homogenize student voices, communities of students like KUL find ways to counter subtractive schooling. For K–12 classrooms, the film offers a window into the anxieties of assessment while prompting discussion about assessment and what it does and does not measure.

To accurately assess our students, we must first listen to them, their stories, and how assessment has shaped their perceptions of themselves and their communities—and then we must share this message. Assessing outcomes from bilingual community engagement, however, means taking a creative approach that accounts for the ways students develop and gain knowledge over time. In student-led projects that extend over a series of weeks, assessment must occur at regular intervals, at points where students receive feedback and renegotiate group roles. The teacher's role in such projects would be to design pathways for students to focus their research and composition on project developments, and to work with groups of students to establish expectations and guidelines based on the project's purpose, audience, and languages. Assessment by both students and teachers would take an evolving approach, with charted points along the way, documenting successes as well as opportunities for improvement. Such project-based learning is both an effective and an enjoyable way to explore community through writing.[4]

No doubt, communities and educators can and do share important perspectives on local and national conversations about homework, testing, competition, and language learning. Community programs can draw upon the expertise of K–12 educators to carefully and strategically examine the assessments that underlie school bilingual policies, including testing methods, instruction materials, and summative assessment models. In a nation of committed educators who envision social justice and grassroots community-building at the center of schooling (rather than the competitive atmosphere created by the present focus on standardized assessments), I think the future will prove that groups of youth who attend programs like KUL and VBL will fill their elders' shoes and continue to find communities as they age, and that many of these students will continue to maintain connections and friendships established in elementary school through high school, college, and adulthood. With collaboration from these kinds of community groups, we can create and focus on assessments that connect community mentorship with workshops and training for academic success, and that stress the value of bilingualism for sustaining community histories—rather than maintaining a limited and limiting focus on standardized tests. As Ofelia García aptly puts it in "American Multilingualism for a Global Future," "policy-makers, educators, parents and communities have to be able to collaborate and trust each other if we are going to raise a generation of bilingual Americans" (309). In the next chapter, I turn to three high school teachers committed to collaborating with bilingual communities through writing.

Chapter Six

Reaching Outward: Teachers Sharing Community Literacies

Taking a translingual stance in our pedagogies means coming to understand the communities where we teach. There are a number of ways educators can learn from the communities of our students and, thus, begin the work of becoming students of our students. As educators, our past experiences as students greatly affect how we look at our own literacies and how we each arrived at the teaching profession. Many of us also have histories of learning new languages, and likewise, these stories affect how we understand bilingual students' learning. However, we may fail to consider not only how our stories affect students, but also how their stories affect us, and how, together, we become characters in a larger story.

I advocate a translingual pedagogy that aims to gather shared insights from conversations and experiences with emergent bilingual communities (Martínez et al.). This mutual knowledge guides us across languages, cultures, and institutions. In classrooms, educators who recognize the emergent bilingual repertoires of young writers can organize assignments and units that encourage students to engage their home languages, translate, paraphrase, and code-switch, calling attention to language differences for discussion and analysis (Orellana; Song; Zapata and Tropp Laman). The translingual view may remain unpopular with English Only purists, but for immigrant families, it legitimizes their emergent bilingualism and acknowledges their hybrid nature.

In terms of encouraging family involvement with community literacy projects, the largest obstacle teachers face is finding time to engage parents outside of school hours. The easiest way to overcome this is to research and reach out to local after-school programs and community centers that offer bilingual assistance, thus fostering relationships with community liaisons who share similar educational motives. This is easier said than done, but strong links between community organizations, schools, and families are necessary for keeping all parties informed about educational opportunities and community-building projects.

This deep form of *confianza* is what Linda Denstaedt, Laura Jane Roop, and Stephen Best describe as *earned trust* in their book *Doing and Making Authentic Literacies*. This type of partnership is based on mutual care and is established over time: "Quality partnerships cause the partners to gain knowledge of each other's strengths, areas of struggle, expertise, and life stories. In that process, trust is earned over time" (105). As Ms. Brice, Ms. Gordon, and Ms. Mason demonstrate in this chapter, accountability, consistency, and care are essential for educators who engage with issues of social justice to earn the trust of communities. Connecting with communities and understanding their strengths makes language arts pedagogy stronger, with curricula that are more relevant to communities' languages and literacy practices. For these three teachers, communicating with KUL members became a way to share literacies and support their students.

In this chapter, I focus on the voices of Ms. Brice, Ms. Gordon, and Ms. Mason and how these educators value bilingual students' out-of-school experiences on their own terms. I analyze three texts by these educators that were published in the KUL student writing anthology. Ms. Brice's autobiographical piece explores aspects of her experience abroad as an undergraduate that inspired her to become a Spanish teacher. Ms. Gordon's nonfiction text is written directly to KUL students, rallying them to celebrate difference and identity. Finally, Ms. Mason's poem depicts the xenophobic rhetoric of a nation divided on the question of immigration. I end the chapter with a discussion about safe spaces, teachable moments of cultural collision, and how Ms. Brice, Ms. Gordon, and Ms. Mason built community *confianza* through a growing awareness of language, identity, and local issues of social justice. The KUL after-school club strengthened these teachers' commitment to emergent bilingual students and the links they formed outside of schools, allowing them to have in-depth discussions with students on a human level they would not ordinarily experience during class.

Ms. Brice: "By Learning a New Language, I Was Also Learning a New Culture"

I begin this section with words from Ms. Brice, a Spanish teacher and cosponsor of the KUL after-school club, and the story of what compelled her to become bilingual. Though not Latina by ethnicity, Ms. Brice discovered a love for Latin American culture in college, which, combined with her desire to be a teacher, set her on a path toward teaching Spanish and becoming a mentor for Latino/a and Latin American immigrant students. Ms. Brice contributed the following text to the KUL anthology:

I grew up in a small town where the most diverse person was the woman who had done the "unforgivable" and had a baby with her Black boyfriend. I lived a sheltered life where the only color was white. In this small town in Eastern Kentucky, no one was bilingual. I went through twelve years of school without a foreign language and feeling scared of the diversity that existed outside of the small bubble we had created. When I went away to college, I was in shock at how many different people there were, and I was somewhat scared of the fact that I was no longer in the safety of my hometown. For me at this time, foreign was scary.

It didn't help that I had to take Spanish class. I had made it through 18 years of my life only speaking English. Bilingualism wasn't something anyone considered where I grew up. The folks in my town were more the "Why don't they just learn English?" variety. But nonetheless I struggled through my first year of college-level Spanish classes in order to fulfill my university studies foreign language requirement. I struggled, and improved, but I realized I wanted to learn more Spanish as it began to interest me. During my second semester, I learned about an opportunity to learn Spanish in Mexico. On a whim, I went for it. I wanted to see more of the world and to practice what I learned.

Upon arriving in Mexico, I was numb to everything around me, and for a few days I struggled with the differences. As time went on, I began to adjust and realized that what I once saw as differences were really likenesses. In Mexico, I met caring people in a community that resembled mine in Kentucky. I came to know people who were striving to take care of their families, willing to help no matter what. I realized that I loved the Mexican culture and the importance Mexicans gave to family. My eyes were opened to the rewards of learning Spanish, and how just by learning a new language, I was also learning a new culture that I have been accepted into with open arms. After many days, years, and tears in Mexico, I am now a Spanish teacher and I get to share my love of the Spanish language and culture and hopefully plant the seed of acceptance that was planted in me during my time in Mexico.

I have always said that I have the best job in the world. I get to wake up every morning and do something not because I have to, but because I want to. During my time here, I have not only fulfilled my life's calling, but I have also taught some of the most amazing students I have ever met. The highlight of my week comes each

Wednesday when I meet with the Kentucky United Latinos. They are a fantastic group of students who will be something great. They are all going to go on to do beautiful things in this world. I know that each one of these students will change the world in their own special way. In twenty years when I look back on these times, I will see that Kentucky is better because of the differences that they made.

Originally from the Appalachian region of Kentucky, Ms. Brice writes candidly about the firm lines of racial segregation in her rural hometown, where "the most diverse person was the woman who had done the 'unforgivable' and had a baby with her Black boyfriend." The strong tone turns from condemning this minoritizing view of diversity in her hometown to describing the sense of loss she experienced as she first began to expand her sense of interpersonal diversity in the world. Ms. Brice points out that she "lived a sheltered life where the only color was white" and links her perceptions of racial intolerance in her community with monolingual English. That she graduated high school with honors without taking a foreign language course indicates the English Only values that permeated Ms. Brice's education. As she notes, her hometown imagined itself as monolingual and unwelcoming to bilingualism: "Bilingualism wasn't something anyone considered where I grew up. The folks in my town were more the 'Why don't they just learn English?' variety." In order to fulfill her foreign language requirement in college, Ms. Brice opted for Spanish, and she struggled. Nevertheless, she found a deep love for Mexican culture, the Spanish language, and becoming bilingual. She valued these rewards enough to study Spanish abroad, putting her linguistic repertoire to the test.

Thinking back to the film *Immersion*, discussed in the previous chapter, we can see similarities and differences between Moisés's sink-or-swim experience and that of Ms. Brice when she studied in Mexico. Like Moisés, Ms. Brice lost confidence in her abilities because of language differences: "Upon arriving in Mexico, I was numb to everything around me, and for a few days I struggled with the differences." I imagine Ms. Brice's self-conscious frustration as she listened deeply to the Spanishes circulating around her, or her "many days, years, and tears in Mexico." Though her home language was not subtracted as Moisés's was, Ms. Brice's emergent bilingualism was not necessarily encouraged either. Bilingualism, for Ms. Brice, became synonymous with biculturalism, and she developed a translingual orientation as she continued her studies in Spanish: "My eyes were opened to the rewards of learning Spanish," she writes, "and how just by learning a new language, I was also learning a new culture that I have been accepted into with open arms."

The transformative experience of becoming bilingual not only drove Ms. Brice to become a Spanish teacher, but also gave her a common ground for understanding the funds of knowledge of emergent bilingual students like Moisés and the members of KUL. Ms. Brice "realized that what I once saw as differences were really likenesses" as she "came to know people who were striving to take care of their families, willing to help no matter what. I realized that I loved the Mexican culture and the importance Mexicans gave to family." Deeply connected to her Appalachian roots, Ms. Brice looked to family as a fund of knowledge, a shared value that she could appreciate as she learned Spanish.

Ms. Brice was a remarkable teacher who learned about bilingual students during her teacher training, and when she met KUL students, she was prepared to support their educational success. Ms. Brice's experiences as a future teacher studying abroad, learning another language, and becoming a member of a community shaped not only how she approached her profession, but also how she understood the experiences of students learning beyond their home languages. At her school, she also led professional development workshops for faculty and staff about cultural sensitivity to Latino/a students. In addition, Ms. Brice regularly volunteered at VBL's homework help program.

Ms. Brice's transformative experience can happen for educators of all subjects and levels. Her voluntary displacement made her uncomfortable but taught her to find commonalities and build community as she became bilingual. Ms. Brice nurtured her bilingualism and shared it as a gift with KUL students, and as an understanding mentor, she listened to students and shared her stories about studying in Mexico, the sometimes-difficult path of learning, and her fulfilled vision of becoming a teacher. In her classroom practices and involvement with students beyond the classroom, Ms. Brice teaches us that taking the time to become members of local communities, and to build bridges between schools and communities, should not be thought of as a sacrifice; rather, it is crucial to connecting future educators, teacher training, professional development, and service learning–oriented courses.

Ms. Gordon: "Your Narratives Are Powerful and an Inspiration for Everyone"

Like Ms. Brice, Ms. Gordon contributed a nonfiction piece to the KUL anthology. Ms. Gordon, a science teacher, did not have the study-abroad experience Ms. Brice had, and she admitted to reading, writing, and speaking only in English. Nevertheless, Ms. Gordon connected to the KUL students in her classes, gaining their confidence, and they invited her to contribute to their anthology. Ms. Gordon's essay reads:

> While we are social beings, opening and sharing of ourselves can be a very difficult and daunting task. We are vulnerable, fragile, and fallible while also trying to be brave, proud, and strong. What others see of us becomes more twisted and open to interpretation and judgments, as value is subjective. Valued or devalued. Accepted or

rejected. Uniqueness becomes weird, culture becomes strange, and strength becomes weakness when you stand alone just trying to fit into a world that sees differences as devalued and leadership as competitive aggression, and not what true leaders should bring as collaboration and support.

When you step into acceptance of diversity and acceptance of self as you are, those around you will also accept and embrace you. How do you become a strong leader while being different? By embracing and sharing all you have to give of your past, present, and future with those who wish to see you reach your full potential. There are educators who understand this, and to the students of KUL, we are with you and support you. Embrace your uniqueness, originality, and your history. Your narratives are powerful and an inspiration for everyone.

Ms. Gordon's text addresses KUL students directly rather than a larger public audience, openly expressing her pride and enthusiasm for the KUL students' willingness to take initiative in their education. Ms. Gordon was instrumental in arranging for college visits and connecting interested KUL students to science, technology, engineering, and math (STEM) outreach projects sponsored by local tech industry leaders and university partners. Without a doubt, Ms. Gordon was one of the teachers throwing opportunities at KUL students, with a vision of these students' potential and positivity toward community service. She learned about KUL from other science teachers who had been involved with members of the group through an engineering club. Though she did not have much exposure to Spanish, Ms. Gordon developed an ear for certain words used among KUL students and the names of different people, days, and events.

In the text, Ms. Gordon shows her understanding of the "difficult and daunting task" of sharing with a community of students learning about themselves: "We are vulnerable, fragile, and fallible while also trying to be brave, proud, and strong," she writes. Her attention to difference comes from a perspective attuned to that of the KUL students. She writes, "Uniqueness becomes weird, culture becomes strange, and strength becomes weakness when you stand alone just trying to fit into a world that sees differences as devalued and leadership as competitive aggression, and not what true leaders should bring as collaboration and support." High-stakes testing for emergent bilinguals, for example, can devalue home languages and the strengths of families. Ms. Gordon offers advice to the KUL students about overcoming this and cultivating their potential as leaders: "How do you become a strong leader while being different? By embracing and sharing all you have to give of your past, present, and future with those who wish to see you reach your full potential." Her words echo those of Ms. Brice in openly discussing issues of difference affecting the confidence of KUL students. With the deepest respect for the dignity of the students and their communities, Ms. Gordon writes,

"There are educators who understand this, and to the students of KUL, we are with you and support you." Her words express the sustained hope of an educator with strong convictions about teaching students beyond standardized tests.

Ms. Gordon was self-conscious about her piece for the anthology and admitted she was hesitant to contribute to the student project, saying, "I wanted to respect their space so their stories could be the focus. I'm honored they would invite me. So I didn't want to let them down."

Ms. Gordon reviewed her piece painstakingly to ensure clarity. After several drafts, she told me she felt confident with what she had produced: "I wanted it to sound just right," she said, "because I know that someday in the future they'll read these words. I want them to hear what I say and let them know I meant what I wrote." Written from her experience of sponsoring the club, Ms. Gordon's text challenges the KUL students to "embrace your uniqueness, originality, and your history." She suggests that in doing this, the students will find the power of their voices: "Your narratives are powerful and an inspiration for everyone." For Ms. Gordon, embracing difference through writing narratives and creative texts is an exercise in staking an educational claim to one's identity, history, and community. The exercise of writing these texts, however, need not only be a student activity. In fact, another KUL sponsor composed her own ethnographic poem to creatively express what she perceived as discrimination against immigrants in Kentucky. Like students, educators, too, can gain from expressive writing that is critical, creative, and illustrative.

Ms. Mason: "Plenty of Opportunities for My Children"

Like Ms. Brice and Ms. Gordon, social studies teacher Ms. Mason learned about civics beyond the classroom and her training as a teacher when she got involved with KUL and, later, became the club's first faculty sponsor. Ms. Mason became a mentor to students by listening to them and sponsoring KUL. Her classroom also became a space where students would congregate before and after school and during lunch. Ms. Mason typically provided snacks for students, that is, when KUL students themselves did not organize potluck events.

Ms. Mason contributed a poem to the KUL anthology. Her piece, "The Welcoming Committee," integrates perspectives surrounding the complex issue of immigration in the South. According to Ms. Mason, this was one of the first poems she had written since she was a high school student. The poem reads:

The Welcoming Committee

What immigrants see
I am going to the land of plenty, plenty of work, plenty to eat, plenty of safety, plenty of
    opportunities for my children.
They say people can work as many hours as they want for three times the pay.
They say my children will have plenty to eat and safe places to run and play.
They say my children will get a better education and graduate from high school someday.
They say the opportunities are endless, just over that border, just over the horizon, just
    across that desert, if I can just reach a little further and try a little harder my children will
    no longer have to struggle.

What immigrants are met with
Don't come across that border, don't come across that river.
Learn to speak English and don't disturb our culture.
Don't muddy our whiteness.
Don't burden us with your problems.
Don't try to teach us about you because we know we're better.
Don't steal our jobs or dirty our streets.
Don't sell drugs and learn what being American means.

Ms. Mason said "The Welcoming Committee" was the most political poem she had ever written. She was inspired to write a creative piece after reading the work of KUL students and coming to learn more about how their perceptions of racism directly affected their ambitions. Ms. Mason wrote the poem from two competing perspectives, both seemingly the views of adults: in the first stanza, the hopeful immigrant parent looking for opportunity and a better life, a sharp contrast to the nativist voice of the second stanza, which openly expresses racist attitudes toward voiceless immigrants—like the one who thinks optimistically in the first stanza despite the xenophobic anger of the second. The exercise for students reading Ms. Mason's creative and critical poem is to contrast the overlapping pronouns of "we"/"us" and "you"/"them."

Before becoming the KUL faculty sponsor, Ms. Mason volunteered to teach at a college preparation summer camp geared toward improving immigrant student attrition and retention rates at the university level. This summer camp recruited immigrant students from across the state to learn about college and build community while staying on college campuses. The camp was entirely volunteer-led, and Ms. Mason became involved by offering to teach a writing class. In this class, Ms. Mason engaged students in discussion in ways she had been unable to in her regular classrooms. "I had never taught a classroom of all immigrant students before," she said. "I was learning so much when I listened, and when I met students from around the state and who were experiencing things that shocked me, but [that] also taught me that my students here were also going through the same things. We all shared stories, all of us. We all laughed and cried, and felt comfortable. It was an eye-opener for me."

After this experience at the college preparation camp, Ms. Mason became better acquainted with the stories of students she knew in her classes, and the constraints they faced. Through dialogues with her students, Ms. Mason became increasingly aware of the issue of stereotypes among immigrants. In my own dialogues with KUL students, I have not been hesitant to talk about this topic, even if it is uncomfortable. For minoritized students, the confidence to share these types of discussions with instructors must be founded on trust and the *confianza* that comes from listening and offering wisdom from experience. Indeed, there may not be answers to any of our questions, but listening is the place to begin.

Though Ms. Mason categorized "The Welcoming Committee" as a political poem, I would instead describe it as ethnographic with rhetorical aims. This poem about immigrant ambitions amid racist constraints captures both sides of the debate. It is ethnographic in its background research, presenting the social context of voices from both sides of the issue speaking to one another. Ms. Mason's poem is based on community research and engagement with students beyond schools; it also reflects on a topic that affects her students, which she learned about from their perspectives.

The topics of racism and immigration connect to what Ms. Mason teaches in her social studies classes and also what she learned by growing up in the South. She contrasts two different perspectives of these issues, leaving evidence for readers to draw their own conclusions. In fact, the rhetorical move of leaving out a resolution to this conflict is a compelling way to encourage more dialogue on the issue. "The Welcoming Committee" became an exercise in creativity and critique, as did all the texts in the KUL anthology. Ms. Mason's poem turned out to be her own contribution to the dialogue of the KUL community, and because of her time and dedication, the students dedicated the volume to her.

Teachers Building Confidence with Communities

Ms. Mason and her colleagues Ms. Brice and Ms. Gordon gained the *confianza* of the KUL students, and when these teachers spoke to students through writing, this sense of appreciation and connection extended into community literacy engagement. Without a doubt, the commitment of these teachers was exceptional. I offer them as examples to aspire to, with the understanding that teachers have lives, families, and communities that take much of their time, which makes that level of commitment to community literacy engagement difficult. For busy teachers, however, there are a number of relevant ways to incorporate community literacy engagement into writing assignments—one way to build connections with emergent bilingual students. The lessons we can take away from these three colleagues are many, but here is a quick list to keep in mind as you read. To learn more about our students' communities, we can:

- Learn about community agendas, find points where you can provide support, and learn how to become active.
- Be respectful of students in discussions.
- Be aware of and reflect on our privileges when meeting communities on their own terms.
- Tutor at after-school programs.
- Explore case studies of students or groups of students.
- Coordinate volunteering by university students and faculty to benefit after-school programs, presenting talks, lectures, and research to families and to schools collaborating with local communities.

Building on the strengths of emergent bilingual communities means connecting them with the substantial resources available to K–12 schools and universities involved in community outreach, multilingual professional development, teacher training, and student mentorship programs for future educators. I can only imagine how Ms. Brice's, Ms. Gordon's, and Ms. Mason's views of bilingual learning would have been changed if they'd had a chance to become familiar with KUL members when they were student teachers.

These teachers' enthusiasm for their students and openness to becoming community mentors shows recognition of the deep connection of bilingualism and culture to the ability to understand a community. Educators who learn to appreciate bilingual communities' funds of knowledge beyond schools learn to connect community values with the resources schools supply, affirming that dignity and education are rights for all. This is also a way to integrate immigrant communities into the social institutions responsible for fostering civic awareness.

As demonstrated in previous chapters, assignments that ask students to gather field notes on language use in their homes and communities encourage the participation of diverse individuals who speak, read, and write different languages. I like to think that anything we ask of students we should be prepared to do ourselves. We can gather our stories, we can create texts that reflect on our experiences of building community, and we can also share these stories with students. In the next chapter, I conclude the book with a call for current and future literacy educators to combine ethnography and creative storytelling. In teacher education courses, ethnographic projects, combined with creative storytelling, can also give future educators opportunities to explore the narratives and languages of students' homes. Students at all levels have much to offer one another when sharing language differences in the context of classroom community literacies.

School Events in Local Community Spaces

Community-driven organizations provide opportunities to interact with communities outside of school and on their own terms, and to find resources for students and families. Consider partnering with local community programs to host school-related activities. Such events could include (but would not be limited to):

- **Back-to-school nights:** Fairs held in community spaces are informative and give educators a chance to get acquainted with local communities. They could also be professional development opportunities for faculty to learn from communities first-hand.

- **Holiday celebrations:** Holidays not only provide content for classes, but also allow schools to participate in local events in community spaces.

- **PTA meetings:** Though it might seem inconvenient to rotate PTA meeting spaces, doing so can encourage the participation of community voices who otherwise might not attend meetings, especially due to a lack of capable translators.

- **Information sessions and informal workshops:** Community programs welcome educators into their spaces to present information or offer guidance. Education-focused programs may find workshops about assessment, bilingual policies, registration, and helpful homework practices especially useful.

- **Parent-teacher conferences:** Like roaming PTA meetings, parent-teacher conferences in community spaces can be a worthwhile way to make direct connections with parents and their communities.

Translingual Pedagogies and Practices in Communities

I start this final chapter with another story—a series of stories, really, this time about an ordinary evening of tutoring at VBL. One Tuesday evening, I volunteered a few hours and helped five emergent bilingual elementary students with their homework, four of whom attended the same school in the *barrio*. First, I helped second grader Allen, who was studying abbreviations for days of the week (*Mon., Tues., Wed.*), street directions (*St., Hwy., Rd.*), and titles of address (*Dr., Ms., Mr.*). After translating each of these into Spanish, we worked on finding proper abbreviations. In order to help Allen understand some of the questions about place names, I pulled out my cell phone and opened Google Maps. We located streets, drives, and highways in the area, noting how the abbreviations looked on the map. Since I grew up in the Southwest, I also showed Allen maps of my hometown in Arizona, with street names in Spanish and English. For fun, we gave Spanish translations to names of streets and locations in the city where VBL was located. Together, we decided that *la calle principal*, or Main Street, was the best place to take a walk.

After I helped Allen, I assisted another student who attended the same school. Third grader Gloria had math homework. The scratch paper she had started in class was covered with fractions and decimals. Together, Gloria and I worked on some long addition and subtraction problems, and I brought over more scratch paper. We each used the paper to work problems out in detail, writing the steps more slowly and the numbers larger in the space across the page. As we moved through the problems, I asked Gloria questions in English and Spanish, while also narrating each of the steps as we did them. Gloria repeated after me and, once she was acquainted with my narration, started finishing my sentences on her own. For word problems, she and I translated words and numbers, again using my cell phone to access the Web to translate terms in Spanish, translanguaging while doing math.

Next, I helped fourth grader Michael with his homework, though this time mostly in Spanish. Michael attended a dual-language bilingual elementary school and was one of the few Latino/a students at this school, which was located a fair distance from the *barrio* in a middle-class neighborhood. Depending on the day, Michael's homework would be in Spanish or English. VBL was the only place in his neighborhood where he could find Spanish homework help. On this day, his homework was in Spanish.

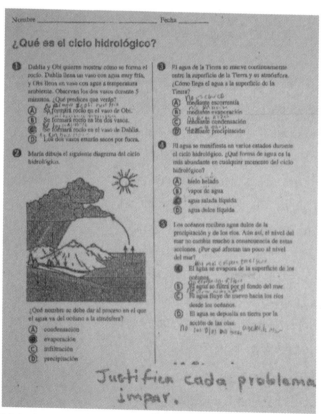

Michael's science homework in Spanish.

I must admit that Michael's translanguaging repertoire far exceeded my own, and I recognized ways I could learn from him. His homework worksheet presented comprehension questions about water cycles. Michael read me the directions in Spanish, then interpreted what he had read into English. After reading with him, I realized how difficult it sometimes was to revise literal interpretations to reflect the intended meaning. Michael asked me for my thoughts, and together we came up with English translations of his homework. As you can see in the photograph on this page, Michael and I wrote explanations for his answers on the multiple-choice worksheet. To help with this, we used Google Translate on my cell phone and conferred as Michael wrote the answers in Spanish. To explain the process of a water cycle, I drew diagrams and extended my Spanish vocabulary as far as I could. I also picked up a few words from helping Michael.

After this, there were no more students with homework to help; however, several students who had finished their homework were reading, coloring, and chatting. I checked in with two friends, fourth graders Lili and Maria. I had helped both with homework at VBL on different occasions. The two were examining an informational brochure from the city for parents registering children for kindergarten. The brochures were bilingual and on display near the entrance of the VBL computer space. I sat with the two as Lili read the Spanish page aloud to Maria. Maria sounded out words with her friend as she read her own copy of the brochure. I also read portions of the brochure in Spanish with pronunciation assistance from both Lili and Maria. Neither of them had younger siblings registering for kindergarten, but both wanted to practice reading. Both had been ESL students in their first years of schooling, and they regularly spoke in Spanish to each other and at their homes.

Seeing this as an opportune moment to read together, I scanned the room for books. I noticed a book someone had left in the homework space, Shel Silverstein's *Where the Sidewalk Ends*. I quickly asked around, and it seemed someone had not shelved the book—to our great fortune. I brought the book to Maria and Lili and asked if they had ever read these poems before. Both shook their heads.

In the previous chapter, I described the ethnographic poetry of Ms. Mason as a model for educators to learn creatively and critically from the dignity of all students and their families, from local voices and communities, and to find expression in writing and artwork. As a researcher, educator, and poet, I have been influenced by this kind of work in my approaches to pedagogy, writing translingual verse, and studying literacy as community building. Based on my experience with Lili and Maria, I composed the following poem about us reading a Silverstein poem, coming from a place similar to the source of Ms. Mason's creative text in the last chapter. We worked as a trio, reading and interpreting a Silverstein poem, translanguaging and engaging in conversation about writing and sharing literacy. This poem, entitled "Fieldnote," attempts to capture the arguments about emergent bilingualism that I make in this book, synthesized into poetic music and narrative movement, illustrating creative and critical translingual writing. The poem also tells a story about bilingual learning, community building, and educational mentorship. I wrote the first draft that evening, after homework help at VBL.

Fieldnote

today tutored
two fourth graders
in tandem, Lili and Maria,
our trio reading poems.
We shared one book
all wondered at an illustration

of two curious children peering over
the edge where the sidewalk ends
perhaps peering into a cavernous gap:
And Maria—"*Ay dios mio*, their *perro* is going to fall."   [Oh my god / dog]
Today: poetry. Everyday: poetry.
Bueno, vamos a leer. Together let's go: [Well, let's go read.]
juntos: [together:]
rhythms bouncing Germanically
to some spot where all roads end
basta ya no más   [enough no more]
no street begins
but some nouns growing *naranjas*   [oranges]
and prepositions *brillando* as crimson crystal   [shining]
y purple *pajaros* resting on conjunctions   [birds]
y los verbos scattering in wind smelling   [the verbs]
like peppermint.
And Lili—"I think the poem is in the fields or the *finca*." [farm]
And Maria—"I think *wind* and *begins* kinda rhymes."
"Yeah."
"*¡Sí!*"   [Yes!]
Trio of laughter. *Juntos pues*.   [Together well]
You like to speak Spanish?
And Maria—"With *mi mamá* and *papá*, yeah.   [my mother / father]
But not with my teacher."
Your teacher *habla español?*   [speaks Spanish]
And she—"*Tries* to speak to me, but I don't
like to talk to her in Spanish
because *estamos en la escuela*."   [we are in school]
When do you speak Spanish?
And Lili—"*Solamente en la casa* or *con mis amigos*. [Only at home or with my friends]
Pero a veces here too when I talk to Maria's mom." [But sometimes]
And Maria—"Me too, when I talk at home,
but I talk to my brother in English and Spanish,
but *más* English."   [more]
And Lili—"And sometimes to *chamaquitos*."   [little kids]
But why do you like to speak Spanish with me?
And Maria—"Because you are nice, and you speak both."
I think I speak more English than Spanish,
como ahorita, verdad?   [like now, right?]
And both—"*¡Sí!*"   [Yes!]
And Lili—"See you are doing it, *eso me gusta*."   [I like that]
Ándale that's translanguaging.   [Right on]
Our last stanza
and *juntos* we stepped slowly   [together]
through the measure following arrows
over rapid lines
back from that grammatical park

ojalá que to someday return   [hopefully]
bringing back *regalos* from another syntax   [gifts]
and dutifully sharing lexicons.
What about those arrows and measured walks?
 And Lili—"Because it's the *camino* to the place   [path]
to see the picture on the front."
Returning to the cover.
And Maria—"*Claro que* yes."   [Clearly]
And Lili—"To the end of the *calles* too."   [streets]
And Maria—"*Pobre perro.*"   [Poor dog]
Maria and Lili formulated their own poem responses,
and they read their poems
as they turned their backs to the gap
at the end of the *calles*.   [streets]
And Lili:
the *parque* is like the forest   [park]
y los arboles son bien verdes   [and the trees are very green]
and we go there on Sundays sometimes
and have *barbacoa* and we visit   [barbecue]

Applause from her audience.

And Maria:
hablo español and English *con mi familia*   [I speak Spanish and English with
                                                            my family]

y mis padres están orgullosos de me   [and my parents are proud of me]
porque tengo buenas notas   [because I get good grades]
y tengo muchas metas y me dicen   [and I have many goals and they say
                                                            to me]

con ganas, mijita porque tu futuro   [with hope, our daughter your
                                                            future]

es nuestro futuros   [is our future]

Applause.

After this I asked
both to write a paragraph
comparing the poems. Maria
sped through her writing
pointing to *español* in both poems
and *familia* at the beginning
of the journey to where the *calles* end.
Lili sighed and stared at her page
and Maria would pause and cheer her friend
and they both finished their paragraphs together
and read them *juntos*.
Lili's mother said *hola* and Maria and I
said *hasta luego* to Lili and then her mother.   [see you later]
I asked Maria why she helped Lili.

"Because she gets mad that she can't write
and read like me. But I like to help her
because she's my friend."
But you don't give her the answers.
"No because the teacher told me
when I help people you don't give them answers."
You like to help people.
"Mostly the little ones. I read to them because it's fun."
I think I know what you want to be when you grow up,
but what do you want to be?
And Maria—"A teacher."

I published this poem for the community literacy journal *Reflections*, an academic publication devoted to community literacy and service learning. "Fieldnote" uses actual transcript quotes and writing from students to give a lyric account not just of the literacy event, but also of the arguments my research emphasizes about the importance of family, community, and *confianza*. I made the choice to write about this event when I thought about the poems Lili, Maria, and I read with one another. Why could I not write a poem about how, as a trio, we read poetry together and bilingually? I recounted my interactions with students on this ordinary night of homework help at VBL in narrative form to begin this chapter, but the ethnographic poem above has a different feel, a different attention to language use and bilingualism, and also a different audience. The interaction became a piece of data for analysis, and also for expression, as I saw another audience for the arguments I wanted to make—similar to my arguments in this book, but made in a different way, with different ends, and bilingually.

This creative and critical reflection includes elements of translanguaging and bilingual dexterity. The transition from this chapter's beginning narrative to the poem signifies that something different is being expressed, aestheticizing the ordinary, but also reliving a moment. As I've emphasized, the interactions represent an ordinary evening of homework help at VBL, just a few hours, but also a wealth of language learning and mentorship, as well as a call to action to make the most of moments of shared learning—similar to the call to action presented by the book you are reading now.

Transforming the notes I took into "Fieldnote" made perfect sense, and the event itself was rich with language play, community, and social meaning. The poem allowed me to further explore the human connection to a literacy event, with students driving the narrative of the text, and also to extend my translanguaging repertoire and poetic sense of creative language experimentation. Such writing also leads me to tell stories, to wander through narratives, giving order to events with the critical eye of a narrator. Creating such texts is important for my development as a bilingual writer, storyteller, and poet, and performing the bilingual experience is also important for my personal growth as an educator committed to translingual research and pedagogy. I enter all communities with a translingual orientation, aiming to form deep and worthwhile connections, open to listening, and equally open to sharing and demonstrating care.

In this final chapter, I urge you, too, to express yourself critically and creatively in your teaching and your writing, and to always value social relationships as the basis for our voices and literacies. I suggest that you connect with bilingual groups in your community. Programs like VBL and KUL are making huge impacts in the lives of students. These programs link students with mentors, safe spaces for dialogue, and opportunities to learn from local funds of knowledge. I end with an appeal for all educators to humanize our literacy pedagogies *en confianza*, to commit to learning from the voices of our students and their communities. When school administrators, the public, and communities of families connect and find common ground, trusting relationships will result. This common ground is based on needs shared by members of the community, and after-school programs are founded on common needs. Families and educators meeting on a common ground share important perspectives on local and national conversations about learning, testing, and schooling. For us as educators, finding common ground is also important as we research and write about how communities personally affect us as members, and as we approach classrooms and community research with sustained care and respect.

Questions for Future Educators

The following set of investigative questions is adapted from Concha Delgado Gaitan's helpful book *Involving Latino Families in Schools: Raising Student Achievement through Home-School Partnerships*. Although Delgado Gaitan presents these questions for educators to ask about Latino/a communities, they can be extended to all emergent bilingual communities. By asking these questions, educators will arrive at a greater understanding of the literacy practices and strengths of communities.

- What activities engage parents with their children/youth after school and on weekends?

- Where do groups hold evening and weekend meetings in the neighborhood?

- What expertise do adults in the community possess?

- Who are the community leaders?

- What community centers are in the neighborhood? What activities do they offer?

- What social networks do parents belong to?

- What bilingual services exist in the community?

Organizing Community Writing Projects and Language Learning in Communities

Throughout this book, I have offered examples of texts from students, teachers, and parents who have formed emergent bilingual communities. I have argued for teachers to engage communities by sharing stories and opening dialogue, and I have advocated for a bilingual orientation that embraces diversity and respect for difference. However, I have not spoken much about my classroom teaching or how I, myself, have integrated many of these ideas when teaching writing.

My writing about community literacy mentorship comes from my own experiences of being mentored as I've grown as a writer, researcher, and teacher. As a mentor, I'm on the opposite side of the mentorship dynamic now, and community has always been at the forefront of my search for belonging and knowledge. I also strive to be a voice that expresses *confianza* in students who might not recognize their abilities as writers, like the mentors who gave me the confidence to believe in myself and my voice.

A translingual pedagogy explores the lived experiences of individuals and communities. Stories are what social life is made of, and when we write with informed understanding, we write about communities biographically and autobiographically. In this way, students teach us what we need to know to actively and meaningfully participate in their communities. As we learn and share stories, we forge connections between communities and individuals *en confianza*, with respect and experience. Over time, these ties develop deeper levels of confidence and community belonging.

Building on the strengths of students and families means connecting them with the substantial resources of universities involved in literacy research, community outreach, multilingual teacher training, and student mentorship programs for future teachers. For emergent bilingual youths, the time and commitment given by older mentors can create a sense of validation, support, and confidence in friendships between mentors and families. Educators who become mentors, regularly volunteer, and share their stories and friendship with mentees are supportive adults outside of schools who demonstrate that schooling is not an individual affair, but rather a family effort and a community project. For K–12 educators who wish to engage with emergent bilingual communities, partnerships of trust are essential to participatory action research, to tapping into networks of individual stakeholders, and to building relationships between the communities and the institutions that serve them. Making connections in spaces like public libraries shows that schools acknowledge that learning happens beyond classrooms, in the civic lives of students and their families.

Educators committed to local communities are conscious that they participate from a position of power and privilege, and acknowledge that they must work to gain the trust of communities through learning projects that show respect for their culture amid structural inequalities (Paris and Alim). That trust can be sustained through a deeper understanding of the social and material conditions facing marginalized communities. Recognizing the dignity of our students' funds of knowledge is critical to understanding the social ties and shared educational interests of their communities, and to building mutual trust between teachers and students' communities.

I remind myself constantly of my duty as an educator to mentor and establish relationships of confidence and trust with students at all levels, to build community by investing in human connections, and to be cognizant of the obstacles thrown at emergent bilingual students. As a mentor, I see the importance of *confianza* as a way to connect students to one another, to faculty, and to opportunities for professional development. Rapport, as I define it in my community literacy research, is trust that comes in the form of two-way learning that disrupts inequalities, and also in the form of literacy researchers' efforts to participate in community practices, learning from the student writers we teach. In my community literacy research agenda and teaching engagement, I am learning about the literacy practices I write about, and my closeness to my communities indicates my respect for and investment in those communities, as well as their investment in me. Investment in, respect for, and contact with communities are of the utmost importance for educators, and lead us to become involved with local programs that affect our students.

Satellite programs that bridge the distance between schools and families are thus primary players in establishing firm links between educators and communities. Out-of-school educational institutions must also be advocates for positive bilingual educational outcomes and school support. I emphasize again that there are programs like VBL and KUL where you live. At your school, students will be able to tell you about local community organizations, some of which may have formed in response to subtractive language policies. The distrust that some families demonstrate toward schools proves the necessity of an out-of-school agent supporting their viewpoints. Educators participating in satellite programs can lend support and credibility to the arguments and perceptions of emergent bilingual parents, raising schools' awareness of the community's concerns and advocating on their behalf. Institutional support translates into knowledge about how institutions work. Emergent bilingual families bring a great deal to the table in schooling situations, and they have the right to make claims and check the power of these institutions.

The Shared Commitments of Safe Community Spaces

Nine-year-old Juana said she enjoyed coming to VBL nearly every day. She participated in VBL's programming throughout the summer months, as well. Her regular contact with VBL staff and volunteers was important for cultivating her sense of community values and pride, as well as receiving English-language mentorship from educators and members of the community:

> I like the homework help, there's a lot of teachers to help. There's kids here working most of the time, so I can get help from them and help them too. There's no people

fighting, and we can get on the computers and have fun with our friends. I also like to read more stuff I learned from school. Sometimes I do storytime and book club because I can have fun with teachers and make friends. We have fun talks and I learn a lot.

Spaces like VBL connect to schools indirectly but importantly, as in Juana's case. In fact, at VBL she came into contact with teachers from local schools who were employed through the library's grant funding to participate in its homework programs. I should note that Juana mentioned VBL as a safe space with "no fighting." The library receives grant funding because violence is so prevalent in the neighborhood, and public programs like VBL have a proven effect in keeping young folks occupied after school. For Juana, this obviously was important, but equally important was the opportunity to make friends, receive language support from trusted teachers, and take part in conversations, sharing lived experiences.

The power of dialogue is in listening and responding, in sharing and building community. Students build community with one another as they share their experiences, their challenges, and pivotal moments in their lives and educations. Sharing stories can change students' lives, while also reinforcing community and academic involvement. Dialogues provide opportunities for sharing stories and wisdom, learning from one another, and participating in the occasional debate, conflict, and perhaps controversy in a safe space where questions can be openly asked.

When schools and communities of families find common ground for safe discussions about language assessment issues, trusting relationships are built. Education consultants, for example, can volunteer to offer workshops for students and adults about assessment, particularly in terms of ELL classifications, explicit language-level expectations, and school contacts. Such discussions can help community programs like the ones I've described, not only by expanding students' academic growth, but also in critiquing how schools shape their assessment practices.

For assessment purposes, educators communicating with students, parents, and community programs must clarify the connections between literacy projects graded for summative assessment. This will alleviate some parents' confusion about, for example, student-led formative self-assessment in portfolio projects. Educators can rely on involvement from communities that share schools' vision for the potential of such involvement, but that organize in spaces outside of schools, such as public libraries and after-school programs. Collaboration between families and educators can allow them to share important perspectives on local and national conversations about homework, testing, and language learning. Educators can invite members of community programs to observe and participate in classrooms, offer presentations, and attend school meetings, while also securing proper language translation and interpretation services. Finally, educators must challenge English Only policies that keep our bilingual students from achieving their full potential.

I end this book by making an appeal to you all, *en confianza*—an appeal to foster relationships through sustained mentorship based on trust. Such relationships are built by sharing conversations, stories, and hardships. I want to point out four predictors of emergent bilingual student success. All emergent bilingual students deserve

1. quality mentorship relationships that are meaningful for both mentees and mentors;
2. institutional support to ensure their future success and bilingual development;
3. opportunities for recognizing and exercising their linguistic repertoires; and
4. bilingual spaces for communicating with other students who share similar experiences.

These four factors shape the success of emergent bilingual students and can result in pivotal moments that transform their orientations toward academic achievement. Such pivotal moments can open academic pathways, helping students envision themselves and their trajectories: where they are now, where they want to be, and how they can draw from the strengths of their communities to build a future.

Notes

1. Names of all participants and programs are pseudonyms.

2. I use the term *language-minoritized* in order to emphasize the process of marginalization that marks the languages of some communities. Though use of *language-minoritized* does not necessarily repair the damages of socially ostracizing individuals who do not speak, read, or write the dominant language, the term focuses attention on the attitudes toward language that mark individuals, rather than treating minority status as part of a group's identity.

3. An excellent source for educators to learn more about the issues facing undocumented students is the national organization United We Dream (www.unitedwedream.org). UWD provides information for undocumented immigrants about rights, laws, organizing, and contacting local support services.

4. The Buck Institute for Education (www.bie.org) creates, gathers, and shares instructional practices and materials (including lesson and unit plans) related to project-based learning for educators of all levels in a range of disciplines.

Annotated Bibliography: Recommended Readings for Teachers

Books and Reports

García, Ofelia, Susana Ibarra Johnson, and Kate Seltzer

The Translanguaging Classroom: Leveraging Student Bilingualism for Learning
Philadelphia: Caslon, 2016.

The Translanguaging Classroom offers practical assistance on how to use translanguaging to help emergent bilingual students learn. This useful book is an important resource that details research and practice for engaging bilingual students in language arts classrooms. *The Translanguaging Classroom* is based on a translanguaging guide for K–12 educators developed by the City University of New York–New York State Initiative on Emergent Bilinguals and funded by the New York State Education Department. The methods in this book have been adopted by bilingual-conscious teachers in K–12 language arts classrooms across the nation.

Krogstad, Jens Manuel, Renee Stepler, and Mark Hugo Lopez

English Proficiency on the Rise among Latinos: U.S. Born Driving Language Changes
Pew Research Center, 12 May 2015.
www.pewhispanic.org/2015/05/12/english-proficiency-on-the-rise-among-latinos/

English Proficiency on the Rise among Latinos examines language use trends since 1980 among the US Latino/a population. The report focuses on home language practices of Latinos/as in relation to demographic and economic trends seen in US census data. As the report notes, the language loss connected to immigration for Latinos/as is similar to that experienced by various US immigrant groups historically.

Library Services for Immigrants: A Report on Current Practices
U.S. Citizenship and Immigration Services / Institute of Museum and Library Services, 2007.
www.uscis.gov/sites/default/files/USCIS/Office%20of%20Citizenship/Citizenship%20Resource%20Center%20Site/Publications/G-1112.pdf.

This report identifies best practices and other useful ideas related to library services for immigrant communities. With examples and suggested strategies, the report offers a short guide illustrating the importance of libraries as welcoming literacy spaces for immigrant families and communities.

Orellana, Marjorie Faulstich

Translating Childhoods: Immigrant Youth, Language, and Culture
New Brunswick, NJ: Rutgers University Press, 2009.

Translating Childhoods captures the voices of immigrant youth coming to terms with translation and interpretation in their everyday literacy practices among their families. Orellana explains the translanguaging practice of language brokering in contexts of families learning to navigate life bilingually. This important work is a fantastic introduction to Orellana's important research, which remains on the leading edge of efforts to understand the funds of knowledge of immigrant families.

Shin, Sarah J.

Bilingualism in Schools and Society: Language, Identity, and Policy
New York: Routledge, 2013.

Bilingualism in Schools and Society is an introduction to the sociocultural aspects of bilingualism in schools. This book presents a research-based examination of the educational advantages and constraints of living between languages. Shin gives an overview of a broad range of sociolinguistic and political issues surrounding the bilingual practices of students in a globalized world, as well as practical advice on raising bilingual children.

Documentary Journalism

Agustin, Amanda
"What It's Like to Be a Translator"
Youth Radio, 24 July 2016.
https://youthradio.org/journalism/education/what-its-like-to-be-a-translator/

This short documentary memoir describes the reporter's role as translator for her mother. Agustin reflects on the frustrations she felt when she was younger and how she came to view her mother's struggles with learning English later as an adult. Agustin's sense of family duty as an emergent bilingual child illustrates the lessons learned from research on translanguaging in family contexts.

Castillo, Marisol
"A Child's English Skills Are a Lifeline for Some Immigrant Families"
Young Reporters, Minnesota Public Radio, 6 Jan. 2015.
www.mprnews.org/story/2015/01/06/young-reporters-children-hold-english-language-literacy-keys-for-families

Castillo describes taking on bilingual responsibilities for her immigrant family as she grew up. Her narrative weaves her voice together with her mother's as they both reflect on the importance of bilingual children for immigrant families. The piece captures the complexities of growing up bilingual for immigrant children, as well as the pressures parents face as they turn to their children for language assistance.

Giaever, Bianca
"What's Going On in There?"
This American Life, 18 Sept. 2015.
www.thisamericanlife.org/radio-archives/episode/567/whats-going-on-in-there?act=2#play

This portion of the radio show/podcast *This American Life* focuses on the story of the language barriers between a father and son. After assuming their son would learn Chinese at home, the parents in the documentary come to realize they've lost the opportunity to cultivate bilingualism for their child. Their son, as a result, becomes English-dominant. After turning away from his father due to their inability to communicate with one another, he attempts to make conversation after 20 years. Giaever's documentary emotionally portrays the intense feelings connected to language, family, and identity. It also illustrates how, despite a language divide, father and son find ways to communicate with one another by translanguaging.

Jauregui, Antony
"Kids Interpreting Medical Information to Parents"
Youth Radio, NPR, 19 May 2006.
www.npr.org/templates/story/story.php?storyId=5418069

Jauregui reports on a bill before the California legislature that would have prohibited the practice of using children as translators for their immigrant parents in medical situations. The piece contextualizes the pressures of emergent bilingual youth speaking between and for adults. Jauregui's piece also captures the reasons why parents may prefer their children as translators.

Jimenez, Mayra
"Banking Translated"
Youth Radio, PRX, 2010.
https://beta.prx.org/stories/43406

From the perspective of a young emergent bilingual journalist, "Banking Translated" explores the complexities of language brokering for parents in different adult situations. The report gives insight into the negotiations of emergent bilingual students and especially the pressures young translators face. Jimenez points out that young people who language broker give voice to their parents and develop a sense of family responsibility.

Bilingual Spoken-Word Poetry

These four recordings of spoken-word performances display the bilingual repertoires of poets translanguaging in verse. Each touches on language, identity, racism, family, and education:

Castello, Erica
"Spanglish"
YouTube, Stanford Spoken Word, 23 Apr. 2012, www.youtube.com/watch?v=iZqDOxW7aG4

Frohman, Denice
"Accents"
YouTube, 30 Dec. 2013, www.youtube.com/watch?v=qtOXiNx4jgQ&index=9

Gómez, Carlos Andrés
"Juan Valdez"
YouTube, 7 May 2010, www.youtube.com/watch?v=Zprgz-qF2Ok

Lozada-Oliva, Melissa
"My Spanish"
YouTube, Button Poetry, 6 July 2015, www.youtube.com/watch?v=fE-c4Bj_RT0

Recommended Journals

Practitioner journals that regularly feature articles addressing bilingual learning and community literacies:

English Journal (National Council of Teachers of English)

Language Arts (National Council of Teachers of English)

Perspectives (National Association for Bilingual Education)

Reading Horizons: A Journal of Literacy and Language Arts (Western Michigan University)

Voices from the Middle (National Council of Teachers of English)

Research journals that feature articles addressing pedagogical practices and bilingual student learning:

Bilingual Research Journal (National Association for Bilingual Education)

Community Literacy Journal (DePaul University and University of Arizona)

International Journal of Bilingual Education and Bilingualism (Taylor and Francis)

International Multilingual Research Journal (Taylor and Francis)

Journal of Literacy Research (SAGE Publications)

Research in the Teaching of English (National Council of Teachers of English)

TESOL Journal (TESOL International Association)

Translation and Translanguaging in Multilingual Contexts (John Benjamins Publications)

Works Cited

Alvarez, Steven. "Brokering the Immigrant Bargain: Second-Generation Immigrant Youth Negotiating Transnational Orientations to Literacy." *Literacy in Composition Studies*, vol. 3, no. 3, 2015, pp. 25–47.

———. "Fieldnote." *Reflections: Public Rhetoric, Civic Writing and Service Learning*, vol. 13, no. 1, Fall 2013, pp. 94–98.

———. "Translanguaging *Tareas*: Emergent Bilingual Youth as Language Brokers for Homework in Immigrant Families." *Language Arts*, vol. 91, no. 5, May 2014, pp. 326–39.

Anzaldúa, Gloria. "How to Tame a Wild Tongue." *Borderlands/La Frontera: The New Mestiza.* 3rd ed., Aunt Lute Books, 2007, pp. 75–86.

Canagarajah, A. Suresh. "Negotiating Translingual Literacy: An Enactment." *Research in the Teaching of English*, vol. 48, no. 1, August 2013, pp. 40–67.

———. *Translingual Practice: Global Englishes and Cosmopolitan Relations.* Routledge, 2013.

Corral, Eduardo C. "To a Jornalero Cleaning Out My Neighbor's Garage." *Slow Lightning.* Yale UP, 2012, pp. 61–62.

Delgado Gaitan, Concha. *Involving Latino Families in Schools: Raising Student Achievement through Home-School Partnerships.* Corwin Press, 2004.

Denstaedt, Linda, et al. *Doing and Making Authentic Literacies.* National Council of Teachers of English, 2014. Principles in Practice.

English Language Learners: A Policy Research Brief. National Council of Teachers of English and James R. Squire Office of Policy Research, 2008, www.ncte.org/library/NCTEFiles/Resources/ PolicyResearch/ELLResearchBrief.pdf. Accessed 28 Feb. 2017.

Fecho, Bob. *Writing in the Dialogical Classroom: Students and Teachers Responding to the Texts of Their Lives.* National Council of Teachers of English, 2011. Principles in Practice.

Fisher, Maisha T. *Writing in Rhythm: Spoken Word Poetry in Urban Classrooms.* Teachers College P, 2007.

García, Ofelia. "American Multilingualism for a Global Future: Recommendations for Parents, Educators and Policy-Makers." *Bilingual Community Education and Multilingualism: Beyond Heritage Languages in a Global City*, edited by García et al., Multilingual Matters, 2013, pp. 309–14.

García, Ofelia, and Li Wei. *Translanguaging: Language, Bilingualism and Education.* Palgrave Macmillan, 2014.

González, Norma, et al., editors. *Funds of Knowledge: Theorizing Practices in Households, Communities, and Classrooms.* Routledge, 2005.

Gonzales, Rodolfo. "I am Joaquín." *Message to Aztlán: Selected Writings of Rodolfo "Corky" Gonzales*, edited by Antonio Esquibel, Arte Público Press, 2001, pp. 16–31.

Hirsch, Barton J., et al. *After-School Programs for High School Students: An Evaluation of After School Matters.* Northwestern University School of Education and Social Policy, Jun. 2011, http:// www.sesp.northwestern.edu/docs/publications/ 1070224029553e7f678c09f.pdf. Accessed 9 Sep. 2016.

Horner, Bruce, et al. "Toward a Multilingual Composition Scholarship: From English Only to a Translingual Norm." *College Composition and Communication*, vol. 63, no. 2, Dec. 2011, pp. 269–300.

Kuhn, Annette. "Photography and Cultural Memory: A Methodological Exploration." *Visual Studies*, vol. 22, no. 3, 2007, pp. 283–92.

Levien, Richard, director. *Immersion.* Widdershins Film / Don't Foam, 2009, www.immersion film.com. Accessed 9 Sep. 2016.

Louie, Vivian. *Keeping the Immigrant Bargain: The Costs and Rewards of Success in America.* Russell Sage Foundation, 2012.

Marrow, Helen B. *New Destination Dreaming: Immigration, Race, and Legal Status in the Rural American South.* Stanford UP, 2011.

Martínez, Ramón Antonio. "Reading the World in *Spanglish*: Hybrid Language Practices and Ideological Contestation in a Sixth-Grade English Language Arts Classroom." *Linguistics and Education*, vol. 24, no. 3, Sept. 2013, pp. 276–88.

Martínez, Ramón Antonio, et al. "Unpacking Ideologies of Linguistic Purism: How Dual Language Teachers Make Sense of Everyday Translanguaging." *International Multilingual Research Journal*, vol. 9, no. 1, 2015, pp. 26–42.

Monzó, Lilia D., and Robert Rueda. "Shaping Education through Diverse Funds of Knowledge: A Look at One Latina Paraeducator's Lived Experiences, Beliefs, and Teaching Practice." *Anthropology & Education Quarterly*, vol. 34, no. 1, 2003, pp. 72–95.

Mora, Pat. "Legal Alien." *Chants*, Arte Público Press, 2nd ed., 1994, p. 60.

NCTE ELL Task Force. *NCTE Position Paper on the Role of English Teachers in Educating English Language Learners (ELLs)*. National Council of Teachers of English, April 2006.

Opitz, Michael F., and Lindsey M. Guccione. *Comprehension and English Language Learners: 25 Oral Reading Strategies That Cross Proficiency Levels*. Heinemann, 2009.

Orellana, Marjorie Faulstich. *Translating Childhoods: Immigrant Youth, Language, and Culture*. Rutgers UP, 2009.

Paris, Django. *Language Across Difference: Ethnicity, Communication, and Youth Identities in Changing Urban Schools*. Cambridge UP, 2011.

Paris, Django, and H. Samy Alim. "What Are We Seeking to Sustain through Culturally Sustaining Pedagogy? A Loving Critique Forward." *Harvard Educational Review*, vol. 84, no. 1, Spring 2014, pp. 85–100.

Rhodes, Jean E. *Stand By Me: The Risks and Rewards of Mentoring Today's Youth*. Harvard UP, 2002.

Rhodes, Jean, and Sarah Ryan Lowe. "Youth Mentoring and Resilience: Implications for Practice." *Child Care in Practice*, vol. 14, no. 1, 2008, pp. 9–17.

Rich, Brian L., and Marta Miranda. "The Sociopolitical Dynamics of Mexican Immigration in Lexington, Kentucky, 1997 to 2002: An Ambivalent Community Responds." *New Destinations: Mexican Migration in the United States*, edited by Víctor Zúñiga and Rubén Hernández-León, Russell Sage Foundation, 2005, pp. 187–219.

Smith, Robert Courtney. *Mexican New York: Transnational Lives of New Immigrants*. U of California P, 2006.

Song, Kwangok. "Nurturing Young Children's Biliteracy Development: A Korean Family's Hybrid Literacy Practices at Home." *Language Arts*, vol. 93, no. 5, May 2016, pp. 341–53.

Standards for the Assessment of Reading and Writing. Rev. ed, National Council of Teachers of English and International Reading Association, 2009, www.ncte.org/standards/assessmentstandards. Accessed 28 Feb. 2017.

Suárez-Orozco, Carola, et al. *Learning a New Land: Immigrant Students in American Society*. Harvard UP, 2008.

Valdés, Guadalupe. Con Respeto: *Bridging the Distances between Culturally Diverse Families and Schools: An Ethnographic Portrait*. Teachers College P, 1996.

———. *Expanding Definitions of Giftedness: The Case of Young Interpreters from Immigrant Communities*. Lawrence Erlbaum, 2003. The Educational Psychology Series.

Valenzuela, Angela. *Subtractive Schooling: U.S.-Mexican Youth and the Politics of Caring*. State U of New York P, 1999.

Van Sluys, Katie. *Becoming Writers in the Elementary Classroom: Visions and Decisions*. National Council of Teachers of English, 2011. Principles in Practice.

Winn, Maisha T., and Latrise P. Johnson. *Writing Instruction in the Culturally Relevant Classroom*. National Council of Teachers of English, 2011. Principles in Practice.

Zapata, Angie, and Tasha Tropp Laman. "'I Write to Show How Beautiful My Languages Are': Translingual Writing Instruction in English-Dominant Classrooms." *Language Arts*, vol. 93, no. 5, May 2016, pp. 366–78.

Zentella, Ana Celia. *Growing Up Bilingual: Puerto Rican Children in New York*. Blackwell, 1997.

Index

Author

Steven Alvarez is assistant professor of English at St. John's University. His research examines the languages and literacies of emergent bilingual Latino/a communities. Alvarez has a decade of experience teaching writing to students from kindergarten through college in communities across the United States, and more recently in China and Mexico.

This book was typeset in Janson Text and BotonBQ by
Barbara Frazier.

Typefaces used on the cover include American Typewriter,
Frutiger, and Formata.

The book was printed on 60-lb. White Recycled Offset paper
by Versa Press, Inc.

30% Total Recycled Fiber